D1299650

YALE SCHOOL OF ARCHITECTURE

EDWARD P. BASS DISTINGUISHED
VISITING ARCHITECTURE FELLOWSHIP

THE HUMAN CITY, KING'S CROSS CENTRAL 03:

ROGER MADELIN / DEMETRI PORPHYRIOS

Edited by Nina Rappaport, with Aaron Taylor and George Knight

Yale School of Architecture
180 York Street
New Haven, Connecticut 06520
www.architecture.yale.edu

Distributed by
W. W. Norton & Company Inc.
500 Fifth Avenue
New York, New York 10110
www.wwnorton.com

This book was made possible through the Edward P. Bass Distinguished
Visiting Architecture Fellowship Fund of the Yale School of Architecture. It is
the third in a series of publications of the Bass Fellowship published through
the dean's office.

Edited by Nina Rappaport, with Aaron Taylor and George Knight

Design: mgmt. design, Brooklyn, New York.

Cover: Image from the Bass Fellowship Studio,
Seung Hwan Namgoong, 2007.

Library of Congress Cataloging-in-Publication Data

The Human City: King's Cross Central 03 : Roger Madelin/Demetri Porphyrios
/ edited by Nina Rappaport with Aaron Taylor and George Knight.

    p. cm.—(Edward P. Bass distinguished visiting architecture fellowship ; 3)

    ISBN 978-0-393-73247-4 (pbk.)

1. King's Cross Central (Project)—Designs and plans. 2. City planning—
England—London. 3. Architecture—England—London—History—21st century—
Designs and plans. 4. Architecture—Study and teaching—Connecticut—New
Haven. 5. King's Cross (London, England)—Buildings, structures, etc. 6.
London (England)—Buildings, structures, etc. I. Madelin, Roger. II. Porphyrios,
Demetri. III. Rappaport, Nina. IV. Yale University. School of Architecture.

    NA970.H86 2008

    711'.40942142—dc22   2008044465

CONTENTS

The Edward P. Bass Distinguished Visiting Architecture Fellowship Studio was inaugurated in 2005 as the result of an endowment from its namesake, Edward P. Bass (1967 B.A., 1972 M.Arch). Bass established the fellowship to bring property developers to the Yale School of Architecture, each participating throughout a semester as an integral member of an advanced design studio. The fellowship provides students the opportunity to be exposed to the dynamic exchanges between developer and architect that characterize a large portion of contemporary practice.

Bass, who studied at the Yale School of Architecture, embarked on a dual career as environmentalist and developer, sponsoring the Biosphere 2 development, in Oracle, Arizona, in 1991, and undertaking the downtown revitalization of his hometown, Fort Worth, Texas, where his Sundance Square Development combined restoration with construction, transforming the nearly dead core into a vibrant center. In addition, he has helped the Yale School of Forestry and Environmental Studies become a leading force in research and advocacy. In taking on both environmental and development projects Bass was supported by the dictum that is central to this school: architecture is a socially engaged discipline, placing the art of building at the service of grand visions and everyday realities.

The Bass fellowship ensures that developers enjoy a permanent place in the school's design culture. Their presence in the studios complements the discourse surrounding the economics and politics of large-scale urbanism and property development that already takes place in many of our lecture courses and seminars. By enabling developers to work side by side with architects and architecture students in the studio, the discussion about architectural design is reframed, shifting the perspective from the architect's point of view to a more holistic reality wherein the many others who contribute to the building process—consulting engineers, city officials, and especially clients—are given a place at the design table.

The first Bass studio was conducted by Gerald Hines and Stefan Behnisch, in 2005, and resulted in the first book in this series, *Poetry, Property, and Place*. The second Bass studio, in 2006, with Stuart Lipton, architect Lord Richard Rogers, engineer Chris Wise, and architect Malcolm Smith, was documented in *Future-Proofing*. *The Human City* with Roger Madelin and Demetri Porphyrios is the third installment.

Preface: Nina Rappaport and Aaron Taylor *The Human City, King's Cross Central 03: Roger Madelin/ Demetri Porphyrios* is the third book in a series that documents the Edward P. Bass Distinguished Visiting Architecture Fellowship at the Yale School of Architecture. Roger Madelin, in collaboration with Demetri Porphyrios, Bishop Visiting Professor of Architectural Design, led an advanced studio in the spring semester of 2007 that explored with students the design of King's Cross Central, the largest development site in central London.

King's Cross Central is being developed by Argent Group PLC in which Roger Madelin is Joint Chief Executive with a master plan by Porphyrios Associates and Allies & Morrison. With the coming of the Channel Tunnel Rail Link (CTRL)—the connection to Regent's Canal and a complex of historic infrastructural buildings including the Granary Building—to St. Pancras Station in 2007, King's Cross Central is one of the best-connected and important industrial heritage sites in Britain.

Following an introduction by Dean Robert A. M. Stern, this book is organized into three sections, the first of which is "The Value of Design: Character, Planning, and Development," featuring interviews with Roger Madelin and Demetri Porphyrios. The second section, "King's Cross Central and London," summarizes the history and current state of the site and its relationship to the future of central London. "King's Cross Central Studio," the last section, begins with the studio brief written by Demetri Porphyrios and Graham Morrison. A brief overview of Argent's "Design Framework and Guidelines" for the development follows, as well as student planning analyses as the students were presented with the master plan for the first time.

In the first half of the semester, students were assigned several individual sites within the master plan and commenced architectural design. Special emphasis was placed by Demetri Porphyrios on the study of traditional urban typologies, the design of the elevation as a mediator between the public and private realms, and the role of site context in the shaping of architectural form. The midterm-review discussions among students, developers, and architects evaluated the projects based on these criteria as they related to the master plan.

The second half of the semester set apart the organization of King's Cross Central studio from the other Bass studios taught at Yale: after reviewing comments from the midterm jury, the students elected to organize themselves into neighborhood groups based on the location of individual designs in the master plan—the Boulevard, Regent's Canal, Goods Way, and Long Park. The students then evaluated the relationship of their collective proposals to the urban spaces of King's Cross Central. A constant theme of this collective research was the role of architectural character in the development and sustainability of urban spaces. Highlights from the final review discussions at Yale by the jury panel of architects, developer, and planners, including Thomas Beeby, Patrick Bellew, Peter Bishop, Ben Bolgar, Robert Evans, Paul Finch, George Knight, Graham Morrison, David Partridge, Alan Plattus, Jaquelin Robertson, Vincent Scully, and Robert A. M. Stern, synthesize the projects in the back of this book.

The editors would like to acknowledge the work of the students who participated in the studio and who were essential to the creation of this book: Lindsay Weiss, Mako Maeno, Khai Fung, Seung Hwan Namgoong, Sini Kamppari, Rose Evans, Aaron Taylor, and Neil Sondgeroth. We would also like to extend thanks to our copy editor David Delp, and graphic designers, Sarah Gephart and Melissa Levin of mgmt. design in New York.

Introduction: Robert A. M. Stern, Dean *The Human City, King's Cross Central* documents the third architect-developer studio to be conducted at Yale, this time with the developer Roger Madelin of Argent Group PLC, based in London; at Yale, Madelin was joined by architect Demetri Porphyrios of Porphyrios Associates, also of London, who has been a visiting professor since 1989. The studio was coordinated by New Haven–based architect George Knight (Yale M.Arch. '95) who has cotaught with Porphyrios at Yale for the past four years.

This studio partnered the developer and architect with the design of a unique urban neighborhood. Students set out to create a new chunk of London and dealt with the established context of infrastructure and architecture, integrating the new with the old. The students first worked as individual designers and then joined together in groups, each of which tried a different approach. They acted as urban designers and architects carrying forward already approved urban plans developed for Argent by Porphyrios and Allies & Morrison.

Roger Madelin has been a developer with Argent in Great Britain since 1987, having previously worked for a major national contractor and a small private developer. He was made executive director of Argent in 1990 and chief executive in 1997 with large-scale development projects such as Brindleyplace, a commercial and residential program developed in the late 1990s that has served as a catalyst for the revitalization of Birmingham. He was involved in the development of Piccadilly Gardens, in Manchester, and numerous projects in London. In 2000 his firm was selected to be a joint developer of King's Cross Central, seventy acres at the heart of London between and to the north of King's Cross and St. Pancras stations—and the subject of the studio.

Outside the office, Madelin, who cycles to work daily, spends his limited recreational time flying gliders. He is committed to good design, place-making and what he calls the "human city." For his superior sense of public responsibility, Madelin was made a Commander of the British Empire in 2006 for the New Year's Queen's Honors.

Roger Madelin shared the studio with Demetri Porphyrios, who with the London-based firm of Allies & Morrison, designed the master plan for the King's Cross development. Previously, Porphyrios taught an advanced studio that took on aspects of the proposed art college at King's Cross Central. His professional work focuses on the making of place and the authentic use of traditional forms of architecture, which is seen in his Argent projects for the design of two office buildings at Brindleyplace. His academic buildings include the quadrangle and auditorium at Magdalen College, at Oxford University, and Whitman College, at Princeton University. His work in urban design includes master plans for towns such as Trowbridge and Rochester Riverside, in England, and Cavo Salmonti, in Crete. Porphyrios holds a Ph.D. from Princeton in history and the theory of architecture. His books such as —*Classicism Is Not a Style* and *On the Methodology of Architectural History*—are important texts in the discourse about contemporary architecture. In addition to Madelin and Porphyrios, the studio also included David Partridge and Robert Evans, both of Argent, and Robert Allies and Graham Morrison of Allies & Morrison, coplanners of King's Cross Central. Various experts in London development—Peter Bishop of London City Planning, Ben Bolgar of the Prince's Foundation for the Built Environment, Paul Finch of the Architectural Review, and Richard Henley of Arup—joined the studio on the site and in the studio discussions.

To Roger Madelin and Demetri Porphyrios I offer my great appreciation for their dedication to the studio process. They join me in applauding the students who so productively and enthusiastically worked together. I also offer thanks to Nina Rappaport, publications director at the Yale School of Architecture, who with Aaron Taylor, one of the students in the studio, together conceptualized and realized *The Human City*, the third book in a series documenting the work of Edward P. Bass Distinguished Visiting Architecture Fellowship program at Yale.

I. THE VALU

OF DESIGN

CHARACTEI

PLANNING,

DEVELOPM

THE VALU
OF DESIGN:
CHARACTER
BRANNING,
PLANNING,
DEVELOPMI
ENGINEERING

Roger Madelin

Demetri Porphyrios

Roger Madelin was interviewed by Nina Rappaport about King's Cross Central in a discussion prior to the studio.

Nina Rappaport: How did you become involved in development projects and start working at Argent twenty years ago? How does Argent's corporate philosophy, expressed in your "internal attitudes" document, allow you to pursue schemes that "can improve on the built environment; have the potential to become part of a real place; follow sustainability principles all with a trust and integrity"?

Roger Madelin: I first worked for a building contractor, having graduated in building engineering, and became intrigued and frustrated about what happened before construction started and why no one pulled the whole process together from the building project's conception. When I became chief executive of Argent in 1997, I thought I would put down on paper what our attitude to any question would be about development: how we set our business objectives, the way we think about the environment, communications, and overall goals. Our projects have to fit these goals, and we only do things we actually feel are rewarding, fulfilling, and that make a difference, since we are a private company and have a choice. Obviously, we have to make money, and we should only do things where we have a competitive advantage as well.

NR: How did you become the prime developer for the King's Cross Central development project in this long-ignored section of London.

RM: I had been at Argent for two or three years, and we had been excluded from a development opportunity in which we learned that if you have a project idea, you need to make sure you control the land. I had a conversation with the founder of Argent, and we talked about what we would like to do before we die, and we agreed that we would like to create a real piece of city in London where people would go and say, "This is a good place." We got a big piece of Birmingham five years later, but then we didn't feel that we were financially or intellectually strong enough to go for any of the big projects in London until the mid-1990s. At that time, we were aware the land parcels around King's Cross were going to come up for proposals again. In the latter part of 1999, I talked with the agent involved and asked how they planned to organize the project. For example, would they choose a partner in the

Demetri Porphyrios was interviewed by George Knight (M. Arch '95), who was the assistant to the studio at Yale, where they discussed the work of Porphyrios Associates and Porphyrios's own philosophy of the built environment and architecture.

George Knight: You often use the term *human city* when discussing urbanism and urban design issues. Aren't all cities, by definition, "human"? Can you share examples of what you mean?

Demetri Porphyrios: All cities are not necessarily human cities. Cities are human when they encourage civility, a sense of scale and proportion, when they are marked by a sense of place and are conducive to a pleasurable and good life. The traditional city is the exemplar of the human city. On the contrary, cities that are simply calculated on efficiency and profit and have no interest in the common public good are inhuman.

GK: You have always shown an interest in the issue of quality of civility. What is civility in architecture?

DP: Civility in architecture is similar to civility in human and social relations. It is the moderation of the individual ego in the light of the collective community. It is the balance between *moi* and *moi commun*—the balance between the individual good and the collective good. I always stress the importance of civility in architecture, especially today when architecture is dominated by self-centered arrogance. We must realize we will never produce human cities unless we recapture this balance between the individual and the collective.

Buildings of neo-rationalists, mid- to late-nineteenth-century neoclassicism, Renaissance buildings, buildings of the Middle Ages and of Byzantium, and Roman and Greek Classical buildings are but a few examples of the Western tradition of civility in architecture. Civility refers to good manners. It is the same thing with architecture. Buildings with good manners are those that respect their neighbors and their city as a whole.

GK: What examples might you point out in your own work where you have established civility?

DP: Our Belvedere Village, in Ascot, built some twenty years ago, is marked by great civility. The

Piccadilly Place, Manchester, England

proper way, one with a pragmatic, deliverable vision for a robust piece of the city in which the risks and rewards are shared once the project moves through the economic cycles? Would they have that team create a great scheme so the best value would be created? And they said, "That is exactly how we are going to choose a development partner." I didn't believe it for one minute, but when they then asked for expressions of interest, we submitted one and went straight from one of twenty-seven to one of three.

At that phase we decided to stick to our guns, and we said that if you want a development partner to deliver a large piece of our city, the long term is essential. You can't do the master-planning without the facts. First, you need to understand the facts—the legal aspects, infrastructure, social, economic, transport, scale, et cetera—so "all" you can do at this early stage is to propose a structure for a financial deal and set out a process as to how you will go about master-planning the project. The other two bidding teams started drawing master plans and produced glossy images, but we stuck to words and figures, and we were selected. We then spent nine months assembling those facts and set up the constraints to develop the brief. Our team included Demetri Porphyrios and Allies & Morrison architects. We involved them in our "Principles for a Human City," which we published with input from the heritage and planning groups.

NR: "Principles for a Human City" includes goals such as creating a lasting new place with a vibrant mix of uses, finding ways to harness the value of heritage, creating a robust framework, committing to long-term success, securing delivery, communicating clearly and openly—all of which reflect the firm's humanist approach. These conditions to improve and enhance urban life are similar to the internal business principles, which you developed for your staff, but in the "Principles" these goals are transferred to the physical development project.

RM: Yes, I would say that is right. I have never articulated it the way. We set out our own internal philosophy before we set out the business plan, which is exactly the same way we applied the principles to the King's Cross development.

NR: So how are the "Principles for a Human City" different from a regular urban development scheme, buildings complement the beautiful English landscape rather than competing with it. In fact, they grow out of the landscape and thereby enhance it. The village of Pitiousa, on the island of Spetses, is another project where civility was of great importance. When one builds in the context of an existing traditional town, issues of scale, morphology, and urban continuity are of paramount importance. Similar preoccupations are characteristic of buildings we have done in London, as for example completing a terrace in Knightsbridge or Chelsea or building new semi-detached villas in Notting Hill, Islington, or Hampstead. When I walk by them, I am happy to see lay people mistaking them for part of the historic fabric of London.

GK: You have always defined yourself as a traditional architect. Does traditional architecture claim a more civil approach than the prevailing contemporary architecture? If so, how?

DP: I would rather say traditional architecture is civil, whereas modernist architecture is not. Traditional architecture is characterized by propriety and good manners, whereas modernist architecture is by and large full of arrogance. There are, however, a number of modernist buildings that are thoughtful and civil. Some of the buildings of Alvar Aalto, Le Corbusier, Louis Kahn, and Aldo Rossi I love and admire. Some of the research by modernists in identifying new building typologies was a search for a new civility. But after World War II, when functionalism was commercialized, architecture became real estate. Architecture, of course, has always been implicated with wealth. After the war, however, architecture began losing its rootedness in place and prepared itself for its future career in the real estate market.

GK: You have written extensively about character in architecture, yet, throughout the profession, its definition remains elusive. What do you mean when you say "character"?

DP: To me, character refers to the specific qualities of a place or an object that gives a place its distinguishing traits. Character, in that sense, is the specific signature—that which distinguishes and sets apart and through which we recognize something. That is why we say, "This person has character" or "What a character that person is." He has specific qualities that are inimitable. That is the sense of character in Classical philosophy. The Greek *carakthr* is the mark left by the pencil or

Magdalen College, Oxford University, 1994–1998

and do you propose, then, to make an organic city? How do you create a new place so that there is a vital mix and a sense of place?

RM: The most relevant experience is the one we have from Brindleyplace in Birmingham—financially or physically, you can't do it all in one go. We had to make sure each phase washed its face. We invest X, and we get X plus a little bit and then move on to the next phase. You have to maintain flexibility and be open to future potentials. What we found at Brindleyplace is, as you move forward, it leads to other possibilities. So even though the time frame is faster than an organic city, which takes decades to build, you are still experiencing that process of new ideas and responding to the market.

NR: Is this what you mean by the "robust urban framework" in which places can adapt over time to new needs and urban conditions?

RM: The robust urban framework allows for new ideas and building types to come in that you didn't envisage, and maybe the framework didn't allow you to do everything. The frameworks have accommodated change, and they responded. We have confidence the first phase of King's Cross will be an exciting mix of uses. Even though we might have ideas for the second phase, people will approach us with ideas we didn't think of, such as a music cluster, food cluster, or a concert hall.

NR: As a developer, do you want to create a northern piece of London that is seamless? As London is constantly changing, how do you decide which London to create or re-create, or are you looking for something totally new?

RM: When I bicycle around London I recognize the city's character in its similar building heights and the way the roads and public spaces are placed in between the buildings. King's Cross will not be like Covent Garden or Clerckenwell; it will be King's Cross, but we don't want it to feel alien from London. It also will not be like Canary Wharf, which makes you feel you are in Toronto or anywhere. Canary Wharf does a lot of things well and caused a tidal wave of development: it was right for that place at that time, and what will happen next in that area will be right for its time as well. King's Cross is part of central London already, and it is surrounded by existing early development. Some of it has had

the writing instrument. Character is the distinguishing aspect of an expression, a face, a place, and so on. Similarly, the architectural character of a building refers to its distinguishing features. Yet such features are characteristic only in as much as they anticipate the urban morphology, which a building helps formulate or is formulated by. In that sense character in architecture does not point to the exceptional and the bizarre but rather to the normative qualities of the urban morphology of the city.

GK: Throughout your experience in teaching and practicing architecture you seem to have been preoccupied with understanding and engaging the defining characteristics of the places you work and study. For example, when the Yale students visited London at the beginning of the semester, you took them on a tour through Georgian terraces, renovated wharf lofts, Victorian market buildings, public squares and parks, high-tech insertions, and heroic transportation structures. What value does this have for young architects?

DP: People never design buildings out of nothing. The landscape or the townscape within which we work always shows the way forward. When we work on a project we become one with the place in which we are asked to design and build. To build in a traditional manner means the building must grow out of the place to which it belongs. To achieve this sense of place one must consider the morphology, materials, and construction practices of a place.

GK: You have recently finished a new residential college at Princeton University. Is that an example of this appreciation?

DP: Yes. Whitman College is very much inspired by the sense of place of Princeton's collegiate architecture. The references of Whitman College are stylistic, constructional, and cultural. Whitman College does not mimic Princeton's earlier collegiate buildings but extends the tradition to which they belong. Old ideas are not merely reassembled; something new is always built out of them.

GK: Your master-plan proposal for King's Cross Central was not dominated by tower buildings but rather by dense, midrise blocks that define streets and public spaces. Why do you favor this approach as opposed to creating more iconic buildings that could become the signature of the project?

huge challenges, and it has to merge itself not only with the same scale of buildings but seamlessly, to help the surrounding areas. There is no softness in our desire to help make it successful economically, socially, and security-wise—besides, it will also benefit our site.

NR: Do you ever feel compromised that you can't build a design you like? How do you balance the issue of an aesthetic interest with the need to make money as a developer?

RM: We have to make our returns high enough to make more money to do the next development. We cannot spend, say, 50 million pounds on a sculpture that doesn't provide an income. Having said that, there are instances where you can't prove it on paper but can be satisfied that if you spent another 10 pounds to 20 pounds a foot and reduced your profit, in the medium to long term there would be a greater benefit that might make the surroundings benefit. We will support an extra expense if it makes a public good and could put the values up. It is perhaps the best thing to do when the values are falling. There has to be a business benefit in everything we do, and the majority of the time we cannot spend more than our competitors if we are building offices, shops, or restaurants.

NR: What is sustainability to you? Is there a chance that King's Cross could be a model sustainable urban project since it is started from the ground up? Is there a possibility for experimentation with zero-carbon emissions and wind- and solar-energy sources?

RM: Sustainability for us is social, economic, and environmental absolutely together. In our view, you can't separate one from the other and if you do, it goes against our definition of it. There is no point in doing something if it is not economically sustainable, because it can't last. People have to finance it and people have to have the means to enjoy it—physically, financially, and socially. The project will fundamentally incorporate better-insulated buildings with energy conservation systems that use the natural environment, with daylight and cooling, et cetera. The city's policies for the environment were in discussion as we were formulating our plan, so we reached the same point together in terms of local energy generation—utilizing combined power systems within the medium term and sustainable fuel such as biogas. The wind turbines and photocells will do a little but will primarily signal the intent. We hope it becomes a model project but not a wacky prototype, because it has to be economically sustainable, too.

DP: London is not a city of towers. London is a midrise city of five to eight stories. It is even significantly lower than Paris. I don't see why one should change the character of London. There is nothing
wrong with making money, and plenty of money can be made with a medium-rise development of
seven to ten stories. I am not against tall buildings in principle, but I am against tall buildings when
they destroy the character of a city. Tall buildings drain land values and activity in a wide radius
around them. Tall buildings work where there is a high concentration of investment and limited
space—as in the case of New York.

GK: Will there not be a moment when London, like New York, is so proliferated with high-rise towers
that it will be a contextually and commercially viable option?

DP: When the Docklands were built, it seemed as if London had just escaped its own destruction:
a new high-rise city was to be built next to the city of London. However, with Ken Livingstone, the
then new mayor of London who is reluctant to control high-rise development within London, the planning process was deregulated. The sad thing is, local government has no civic ideals but only commercial gain in mind.

GK: King's Cross was once bustling as a food and goods depot, receiving and distributing material
throughout Victorian London. As its utility obsolesced in the late nineteenth century, many of the
buildings and transportation structures were abandoned and then most of them landmarked. Do you
consider these existing historic structures in King's Cross to be an impediment or an asset to such
a large-scale development?

DP: I definitely consider these buildings to be an asset. Over the past twenty years or so many
planning applications and master plans were made for King's Cross. These efforts have failed not
because of lack of investment or lack of architectural talent. All previous proposals had planned
the demolition—partial or total—of the nineteenth-century industrial structures, which they saw
as a liability. We were the first to propose a master plan that said the buildings must stay. I do
believe such buildings are an asset for regeneration, because they give instant character to any
new development. They empower the new with a sense of place and provide a thread of historical

Brindley Place, Birmingham, England 1997–2000

NR: Does this mean you are generating your own electricity and building a powerplant?

RM: Yes, we are generating the full base load of our electricity on the site with a number of combined heat and power-engines which will also provide hot water and distribute water in a district heating and cooling system. This will be part of the first phase, which includes two residential buildings, a new University of the Arts center in the Granary Building, public space, and infrastructure that will connect to the surrounding streets to the canal. South of the canal, around the stations and up to the new canal bridge, we will be refurbishing the German Gymnasium Building and the Great Northern Hotel, and we will be building three new office buildings with retail and restaurants on the ground floor and connections to the north. The first phase will be mixed and have its own public realm and civic space and will be connected to existing parts of London.

NR: In some areas it seems you are functioning as a city agency by building your own streets and sewage systems. What does the city contribute to the project?

RM: We do have in the U.K. an extraordinary amount of freedom. Of course, we have planning guidance from a regional and national level, but within that, how we phase it and what we include is up to us. We have brought the public authorities along with our ideas and if they didn't like it, they would stop us—but it is driven by us. The converse side is that we are providing twenty new streets, public spaces, electricity supplies, and drains at our own expense. One of our partners will be a major electrical distribution company. While we could have a private police force, it will be better if we work with and add to the local police force.

NR: Who will live here, and how do you make it mixed enough so that it follows former mayor Ken Livingstone's desire for 50 percent affordable housing for new developments?

RM: We will have 44 percent affordable housing, and there are lots of regulations for this. For us, what we call social housing is for the lower incomes and will be allocated by the local authorities for a certain number of families and unit sizes, all with a Sustainable Renting Plan in which they agree that they won't put just one kind of tenant in a building. They have agreed that there will be an element of continuity to the city. It is difficult today to build in the robust manner of the nineteenth century, so why would one demolish buildings that withstood their own functions then and can withstand their new functions today? Cities are made in layers of different periods and cultures; the beauty of traditional cities is exactly their multilayered urban narrative. Cities, like families, grow over time, and it is the overlaps of generations and centuries that give character, significance, and a sense of place to cities.

GK: What does sustainability mean to you, and how do you promote it in your work both generally and at King's Cross?

DP: "Sustainability" is not an architectural term; it is a way of life. "Sustainable" is that which ensures the same, if not a better, life for your children. All traditional societies have been sustainable. Sustainable buildings are robust enough and can be reused again and again for centuries. In that sense, traditional buildings are examples of sustainable architecture. The rhetoric of contemporary modernist agendas of sustainability is a hoax. Buildings that flaunt multilayered glass curtains and stainless steel are but an oxymoron. Their passive carbon footprint makes them unsustainable from the start. Instead, local materials, robust construction, and versatile building typologies are guarantors of sustainable buildings.

GK: Can you give an example from your own work in which you have achieved a particularly sustainable building?

DP: A good example is the office building we designed for Argent at Brindleyplace. A steel structure supports the floors and roof, while a thick masonry-bearing wall encloses the building. This is a fast-track internal structure with a slow-track external envelope. Its sustainable building fabric has a minimal carbon footprint, and its masonry envelope has excellent thermal properties. Present-day globalization markets have duped us into believing that building materials can be bought and sold to us from all over the world, like wristwatches. This is arrogant and irresponsible.

GK: Your firm has been developing a master plan for Roger Madelin and Argent's King's Cross

mixing within their own allocation. There will be moderate-income housing as well as public-sector housing for teachers, doctors, and so on, and over half is market rate.

NR: How are you able to successfully incorporate a civic or public space in the overall cost of a development?

RM: The advantage in Birmingham was that we paid little for the site because the market was starting to improve, and we felt it was worth it to invest in a high-quality public realm, quality that no one had seen. It made people recognize what we were doing, so when we produced the office space we would already be on the map. We raised the site price, which was still below market. At King's Cross, we are lucky the two landowners selling us the site are aware of quality. The project is so complicated and notorious that it will take time to change in physical reality and in the perception of King's Cross, which was known for filth and grime. But the landowners knew we had to invest early on in quality; and we did not agree on the value of the site until we were ready to go. We hope not to fall into the trap of most development sites in a strong market: when prices are high and people become optimistic, but then dismiss problems or challenges by thinking it can be done cheaper than the cost of public improvements. Then, because the investment becomes less, the development becomes rubbish because site owners understand the maximum value from day one. Either they just believe optimistic forecasts, or they don't foresee the outcome and have paid too much for the site to invest in the public space.

As a company, we only look for large, meaningful development opportunities, with a sustainable entry price and with owners or city authorities who have a longer time frame; then, they can wait for the best value. It takes a strong politician and someone with a long-term vision. You have to choose your landowners on that basis.

NR: How do you educate your whole team about design? I didn't notice the word *design* in your principles.

RM: In the King's Cross project we have fifty new buildings and one million square feet of heritage buildings. Most of the buildings should be good, well-designed "ordinary" buildings. We do need gems, development for many years, and they have recently succeeded in obtaining planning permission. What has been your perspective on the project, and how have you been able to advance it?

DP: We have worked very successfully with our joint master-planners, Allies & Morrison, for the past six years. Both practices have had similar interest in rational architecture and urban design. Both practices place great emphasis on the importance of the public realm, and that has been our perspective on the project.

GK: With about sixty structures proposed to be built at King's Cross, do you think it is valuable to have a single architect controlling the design, or would you prefer to see a number of architects working together? If the latter, what underlying values would you want to see shared among the designers?

DP: It is like asking, does a king govern better than a number of elected members? To tell you the truth, I do not have a preference as long as one or the other is enlightened. An enlightened king can run the state beautifully, yet at the same time there are tyrants who can destroy public life. Similarly, an elected government can do a great job, yet many disgraceful aberrations have come out of democratic systems. I know one thing: the most-loved neighborhoods in many traditional cities like Paris, London, New York, and Vienna have been created by a single vision. The problem with single visions today, however, is there is no political backing to implement them. It is inevitable that developments today are executed by many different architects, but there are problems with this. For example, when you put thirty architects together it is like visiting a zoo. Achieving a collective morphology for a neighborhood today is one of the great challenges in contemporary planning and urban design. I believe a good middle point is for developers to seek the characterization of selected urban sequences—for example, streets, boulevards, squares, waterfronts—by single architects.

GK: What role do developers play in shaping and monitoring these values?

DP: We have worked closely with a number of developers in England, Germany, Italy, Greece, and the United States. Our relationship with Argent has been exemplary. We always respond to the

Interamerican Building, Athens, 2000–2002

whether they become iconic buildings on an international stage or not. I would be disappointed if we didn't have gems, but it wouldn't be a disaster of a place if they were not all part of the story. There are of course many fine original buildings, and if the uses are correct and the public spaces good, it will be a great place to be. If we have a place for people, the gems will be a bonus. We are now just working at a sketch level with about twenty architects, and another group have contributed to a design charrette.

NR: How do you feel about a project designed by one architect versus developing a plan with code restrictions and regulations, which then guide the design of many different architects?

RM: Instinctively, I am not a code person. I like to think of many people coming together to share a common goal. That is how I run the business. But I think we can get different architects to design these buildings, and it would hold together with the right people in the right environment. There are other issues about making developments, such as how much guidance and how many architects. The development in Birmingham with Demetri and Graham holds together well with very different styles. I think King's Cross will benefit from different hands, but perhaps there can be a similar palette of materials and approaches to frontage and colonnades.

NR: What impact did you want to achieve or have on the built environment? Rather than just as a developer of standardized buildings for large corporations, do you have an interest in innovative design? Do you want to achieve that in the marketplace?

RM: At the beginning I didn't know the answer to that question. I knew it was inefficient in many ways for a building to be built without the builder understanding or being involved in the process of conception. But I soon started to work with architects such as Edward Cullinan; in seeing his projects, such as schools and residential accommodations for special-needs kids, I started to realize buildings and the environment around them have an influence on us. I had always seen it from the very technical point of view—can you get the goods in and out, retail square feet—as numbers. Now that has changed. I think buildings can make a difference by integrating the conception, design, and the environment. It is much bigger than I ever imagined.

requirements of developers, and they have always listened to our suggestions. Argent is tough and always has you on your toes—which is good.

GK: You have often said that, as one approaches an architectural design, "The building must always be smaller than the commission; second, the project is always greater than the commission." What does this mean?

DP: In any given commission the tendency today is to make a single building, a megastructure. But I say you should look and evaluate whether the commission should be broken down to more than one building. That approach helps give a human scale to the buildings. The other thing is that any given commission is necessarily narrow-minded—someone has a plot of land, available funds, and so on. What I mean here is, every commission is defined by the contingencies of its historical limitations. Yet every time you get a project you have to find a solution that transcends these limitations and arrives at a normative solution. When I say the project is always greater than the commission, I draw attention to the fact that every design solution must have a wider application and significance.

II. KING'S CROSS CENTRAL AND LONDON

I. KING'S
CROSS CEN
AND LONDO

King's Cross, Past and Present The history of the site offers many clues about the essence of King's Cross Central today and for the future. The existing buildings and places, many of which are still intact, were the starting point for new development. By embedding new buildings among old, the character and life of each can be shared and the human benefit multiplied.

The two grand railway stations of King's Cross and St. Pancras lie adjacent to the King's Cross Central development. King's Cross Station celebrated its 150th anniversary in 2002, while St. Pancras has the most spectacular train shed of the High Victorian period, including wrought-iron arches spanning 243 feet, designed by C. J. Barlow. Within the site there are seven historic buildings with a combined footprint of over 350,000 square feet. The Granary, at the heart of these historic structures, is the only surviving centerpiece of one of London's major nineteenth-century trade hubs. At one point it held up to 60,000 sacks of corn, with a hydraulic system for hauling the grain up through the building. The east and west transit sheds, attached to either side of the Granary, are of exceptional size for their period (1850s), each being 590 feet long and 82 feet wide. Finally, the Triplet Gasholders are the tallest to have ever been built with cast-iron columns. The round guide frames are unique among gasholders for the three-way structural linkages in which the three frames abut. Underlying the imposing robustness of the site are the raw materials of its past: gas, coal, grain, iron, brick, and stone all played their part in defining the character of the place.

In 1894, two contrasting textures characterized the site. To the south, the orientations of King's Cross and St. Pancras stations were determined by two different grains of urban development to the east and west. This left a triangular fragment of land between the two, the thrust of which followed the ancient River Fleet. This feature has become a bottleneck converging on Euston Road. To the north, the fanning grain of the Goods Yard spreads elegantly to meet the Regent's Canal—a marked contrast to the fragmentation of the south.

Cutting across the north-south thrust of the railways is an older, more fluid element of the site's history: Regent's Canal was completed in 1820 in a cutting along a boundary line between two fields, which created the curve that now defines the Goods Yard. It was built to transport goods,

connecting the Thames to the nationwide network of canals. In particular, it brought coal
to the Gasworks, constructed in 1824.

York Way, formerly known as Maiden Lane, is the oldest remaining feature on the site. Although
it has long been a neglected and inhospitable place, there is an opportunity now for it to become a
major spine joining King's Cross Central to the existing communities to the north and south.

The south area of the site has always had an isolated and confusing pattern, with no obvious connection for people to move northward. Before the railways, it was one of the infamous old-style slums
of London, dominated by a smallpox hospital and the Gasworks. To pave the way for regeneration,
existing grains in the south need to be restructured and a new spirit superimposed on the old. In the
north area of the site, the spreading railway grain would be the starting point for a pattern of urban
blocks. The vast volume of the Granary complex anchors the center of the site, both in terms of geometry and mass, providing an engine house of activity. Additionally, the east-west grain of the now-
removed potato market plugging into York Way sets the pattern for permeability eastward. The four
historic Gasholders are to be relocated to the northern edge of Regent's Canal. The Granary, transit
sheds, Coal Drops, Midland Shed, Handyside Canopies, Regeneration House, and Fish & Coal Building
are to be retained and refurbished at the heart of the development. These buildings are remarkable
for their immense scale, linear repetition, and robust simplicity. This condition, combined with the
more lightweight use of iron and timber that was so typical of the Goods Yard, provides a strong context within which new buildings can be designed.

The King's Cross Central site, outlined in orange, a former Victorian-era goods yard, was one of the first intermodal hubs in the U.K.
The use of the natural topography of the site, with interlocking levels and inlets from Regent's Canal for the transfer of goods from
rail to road and boat, continues to have a major impact on the unique character of the site.

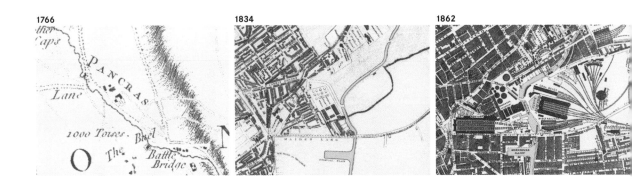

1766

1834

1862

1766 Maiden Lane (now York Way) and the River Fleet
pre-date all developments.

1834 Regent's Canal was completed in 1820, and the
Gasworks were completed in 1827.

1862 By 1852, King's Cross and the northern Goods
Yard were substantially complete.

1894 The Midland Railway Co. completed St. Pancras
Station in 1868.

1999 Prior to the commencement of CTRL works,
many fragments of the Gasworks and industrial
structures were intact.

2007 Once completed, CTRL leaves a site with huge
potential for regeneration.

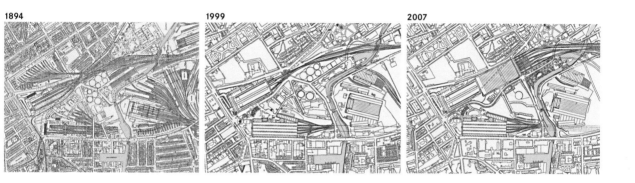

1894   1999   2007

Watercolor signed by Lewis Cubitt and exhibited at the Royal Academy in 1851.

Yale Students in London with Roger Madelin and Demetri Porphyrios.

London's Bigger Picture At present the site is isolated but surrounded by potential links to central London. Two emerging places within the site, Station Square to the south and Regent's Canal at the center, hold the key to giving King's Cross Central accessibility, a unique sense of place, and a focus. What will become Station Square is at present a fragmented and confusing place in need of restructuring. In contrast, Regent's Canal has a lasting and powerful order but is disconnected from everything around it. A simple and bold connection between the two is essential for opening up the site to the rest of London.

From Station Square, two new spaces, the Boulevard and St. Pancras Square, with a dominant north-south grain, connect to Regent's Canal. Of these two, the Boulevard would meet the direct-desire line, with a long view up to the great space at the heart of the site. By contrast, St. Pancras Square would be gradually revealed, part of a second, alternate link to Regent's Canal, thus offering pedestrians a route with a different character and experience. Both routes come back together at the canal. Here, a pedestrian crossing and two new bridges over the canal would interlock with Granary Square, ensuring the canal would no longer be a barrier. These two distinct routes respond to the daily patterns of people moving through the site, many of whom would be going to and from work each day. Allowing people to spread out and filter through the urban blocks of the south part of King's Cross Central would create the familiar condition of a pleasant walk to work while providing diverse and direct routes from place to place.

Regent's Canal is the primary connector from east to west. To the west, the towpath to Camden Town would link to the upper level of Granary Square via the public space around the Gasholders. This would form new connections north and east and to and from Islington via Long Park. In addition to the existing towpath route, a new footbridge over the canal and across the Camley Street Nature Park would connect westward to Camden Town. The Gasholders would be a landmark drawing people down through the grain of new streets and spaces and contributing to new connections between Camden Town and Islington. Eastward, the towpath would be linked to Wharf Road by steps and ramps. These measures would strengthen the connections and create a sense of welcome to York Way and south Islington.

To the north of Regent's Canal a broad fissure opens up between new urban blocks, taking its cue from the splayed lines of the original railway grain. Long Park would occupy the northern section of this natural fault line, which runs from one end of the site to the other, bringing not only connection but unity and resonance to the new urban grain. This central space would be only one of a number of routes connecting north and south, reflecting the prevailing north–south urban grain. Across this grain, Goods Street, the main route into the northern section of King's Cross Central, locks Long Park into existing street patterns to the east of York Way by continuing the east–west orientation of Copenhagen Street across the site. At the north end of Long Park a simple link would be made into York Way by way of North Square, the gateway of arrival from the north. With the considerable changes at King's Cross Central, York Way would no longer be a barrier but be reborn as a spine of activity and connection for new and existing communities. Lateral connections into the site from York Way are crucial to achieving a secondary layer of permeability and interdependency across the site boundary.

The inheritance of nineteenth-century buildings at King's Cross Central is an extraordinary asset. In addition to being the key to a unique sense of place, these buildings provide a series of local landmarks that bring structure and orientation to a complex site. Some of these landmarks are revealed locally as one moves from space to space; others, such as the Granary Building, St. Pancras Clock Tower, and the Gasholders, are seen from a distance. Together, this network of new urban spaces and visual landmarks would create connections both within King's Cross Central and throughout the surrounding fabric of central London.

Yale Students in London and Oxford with Roger Madelin and Demetri Porphyrios.

Aerial photograph of the site, with King's Cross and St. Pancras stations and the newly completed Channel Tunnel Rail Link in the foreground, looking north, 2007.

top left: The Granary Building and current site conditions, looking north, 2007. top right: View of southern section of King's Cross Central from Granary Building, with King's Cross Station and London in background, 2007. bottom: View of Gasholder No. 8, with tower of St. Pancras Station in background, from Regent's Canal looking east, 2008.

Embedded Heritage The existing buildings, their form, disposition, scale, and character, have been central to shaping the urban master plan with its new fabric and public spaces. The new has grown out of, rather than being imposed upon, the old. This concept lies at the heart of the notion of embedded heritage and is an important element in the idea of the Human City.

Rather than setting these buildings apart or putting them into a "museum city," they will be woven into the fabric of the living and working community to facilitate secure and sustainable new uses. These structures add to the complexity of the site, and they are a unique asset of great value. They give King's Cross Central the sense of having "come from somewhere" and suggest a collective memory. They balance diversity and intimacy of scale with an overriding order.

above: Crossroads of King's Cross, the intersection of Euston Road, York Way, Pentonville Road, and Gray's Inn Road, looking East, 2008. opposite: Changing face of King's Cross, St. Pancras Station and the Great Northern Hotel frame Norman Foster's Barlow Shed Extension.

Interior of Granary Building highlights the character of Victorian-era structural systems, 2007.

View of Gasholder No. 8 from Regent's Canal, with King's Cross and St. Pancras stations in background, looking south, 2008.

III. KING'S C

CENTRAL ST

ISLINGTON

Highbury and
Islington

Camden Road

Caledonian
Road and
Barnsbury

Camden Lock

Upper Street

Camden Town

Regent's Canal

St Pancras Ex

Angel

St Pancras Station

King's Cross

10 mins walk

Euston

20 mins walk

EST END

Holborn Circus

30 mins walk

Oxford Circus

Tottenham Court Road

MID TOWN

River Thames

Diagram showing location and connection of King's Cross Central to central London.

The Human City: King's Cross Central Studio Brief The King's Cross Central design studio at Yale in spring 2007 was a comprehensive study in which the students relied on a given master plan prepared by Porphyrios Associates and Allies & Morrison of London for Argent Group PLC. The design studio focused on the idea of character and asked the students at the beginning of the semester if a two-dimensional master plan is a sufficient guide to create a vibrant new urban quarter, or are there any other parameters necessary to define it?

The usual design of a master plan is represented with a physical, figural proposition that addresses issues of social relevance, use, and density, resulting in a heavily prescriptive list of what can and cannot be done. Instead, this master plan is a physical proposal that includes a set of non-prescriptive guidelines, encouraging contributing architects to recognize specific characteristics and opportunities unique to different areas within the development site. That strategy, together with illustrative proposals showing how that plan would look if it were actually realized, established a concept about a specific plan but also fostered a paradigmatic approach to collaborative design based on specific theoretical aspirations. In this sense the master plan was a framework within which individual design proposals could be tested against much broader issues. The idea of civility underpins the non–prescriptive master plan and is crucial to the success of King's Cross Central. "Civility" is here understood as the commitment of designers to a deep and lasting conversation focused on the public realm, allowing for the creation of both individual architectural works of high quality as well as a coherent and sustainable city.

The regeneration model adopted for the studio is based on the idea of the Human City, the principle of which is the long-term sustainability of urban development: maximum connectivity with the existing city, a physical urban plan with low- to mid-rise high-density buildings, and a physical urban plan that establishes a dialogue between public and private urban spaces. The realization of the physically Human City entails the notion that the city has both a macro- and micro-diachronic dimension manifested in the master plan. The macro-diachronic dimension is represented at King's Cross Central in the north-south route that becomes the backbone of the whole south side and is expressed as the intersection of major pedestrian and vehicular axes of the north side, with the public spaces in the very center and large quadrangles within which the streets, squares, and blocks can be developed. Another interest of the master plan is the regeneration and enhancement of the green spaces: parks, canals, and waterfronts. The historic buildings were treated as structures that should be rejuvenated, reused, and embedded within the temporal framework of the new Human City. The micro-diachronic task was to look at the idea of a neighborhood and see how each neighborhood in the site could be given a sense of place. The studio investigated the relationship between a two-dimensional master plan representing quantitative criteria and qualitative aspects inherent in three-dimensional-plan stylistic specificity as developed in the idea of character.

King's Cross Central has an important role to play within London as an international city. The challenge and opportunity is to produce a dense and vibrant quarter that is exemplary for a sustainable world city. The Yale studio asked students to focus on buildings of varied uses, including commercial, office, retail, residential, and recreation, addressing both the design of the buildings and their surrounding spaces. Each student was responsible for the design of three to four buildings. The studio focused on the dialogue between buildings and public open spaces—streets, boulevards, squares, waterfronts, and parks—to give the city character, value, and a sense of place.

The Human City is discovered at the intersection of time, space and form. In it, the social life of Man and the formal life of the City resonate in a complex temporal framework

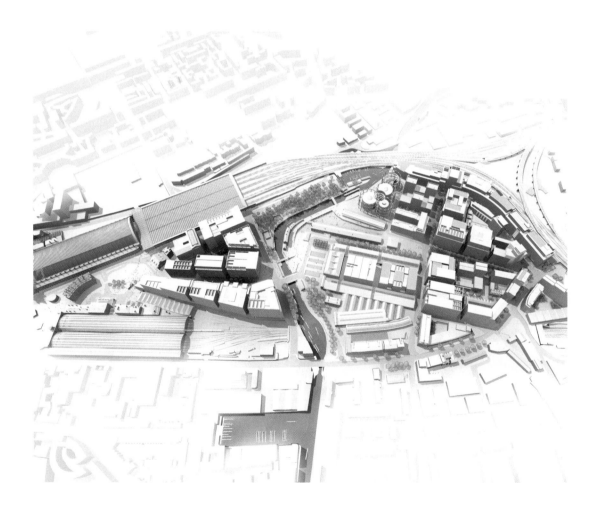

Bird's-eye view of the King's Cross Central master plan as designed by Porphyrios Associates with Allies & Morrison in 2006. The CTRL runs from north to south along the west side of the site and terminates at St. Pancras Station, with King's Cross Station below on the left. York Way bounds the site on the east, and Regent's Canal runs from east to west through the center of King's Cross Central. opposite page: Existing ground-level use around King's Cross Central.

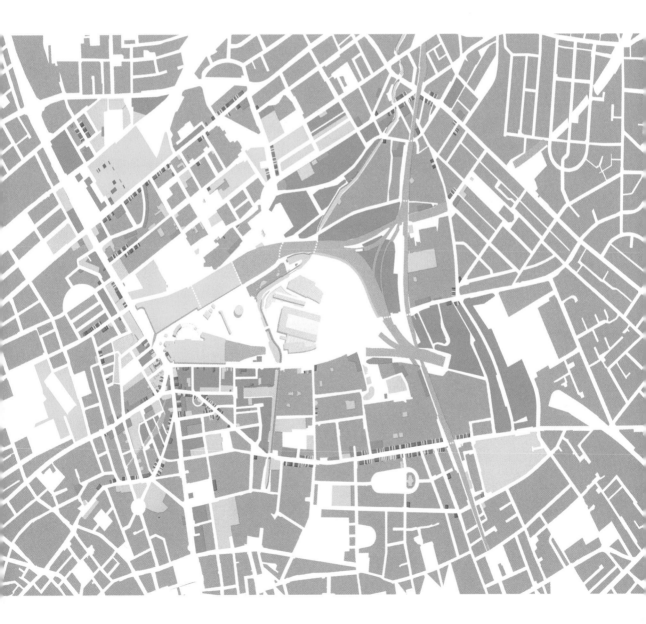

GREAT NORTHERN HOTEL

STANLEY BUILDING
GERMAN GYMNASIUM

FISH AND COAL OFFICES

ST. P
CHU

BRILL PLACE

ST. PANCRAS ROAD

SULTON STREET

BRITISH
LIBRARY

CAMLEY STREET

CAMLEY STREET
NATURAL PARK

MIDLAND ROAD

ST. PANCRAS EXTENSION

REGENT'S CANAL

GRANARY
SQUARE

ST. PANCRAS STATION

CLARENCE PSG

PANCRAS ST

GASHOLDER
NO.8

ST. PANCRAS ROAD

AREA FOR FUTURE
KING'S CROSS STATION
ENHANCEMENT

TREET

KING'S CROSS STATION

FIELD STREET

YORK WAY

MAID

BIRKENHEAD STREET

CALEDONIA ST

RAILWAY ST

WHARFDALE ROAD

BATTLEBRIDGE
BASIN

NTON

The site in 2007: A wealth of heritage and natural resources, but surrounded by infrastructure barriers and urban compounds.

GRANARY ST

CAMLEY STREET

ST. PANCRAS BASIN

PANCRAS LOCK

NEW THAMES LINK TUNNELS

CTRL EMBANKMENT

NORTH LONDON LINE

WESTERN GOODS SHED

ESTERN COAL DROPS

AL DROPS

THE LINEAR LAND

WESTERN TRANSIT SHED

NEW ASSEMBLY SHED

YORK WAY

ASTERN TRANSIT SHED

LAND
D

OLAND SHED

THE TRIANGLE

FORMER YORK ROAD
LUL STATION

RANDELL'S ROAD

COPENHAGEN STREET

BEMERTON STREET

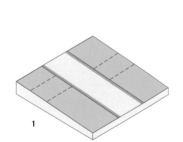

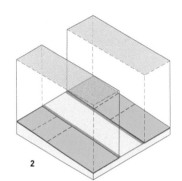

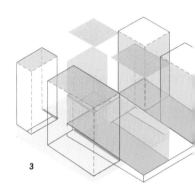

1

2

3

1 Development Specification Development zones and plot boundaries.

2 Development Specification Maximum height limits and overall massing. Floor-space limit above 30m–31m defines massing at upper levels.

3 Guidelines Building lines define edge of public realm.

4 Guidelines Minimum elevation height defines enclosure of space and continuity among buildings.

5 Guidelines Setbacks provide daylight cones and encourage good daylight for buildings and public space.

6 Illustrative Build-out scheme.

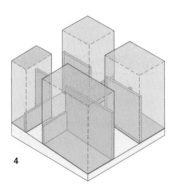

4

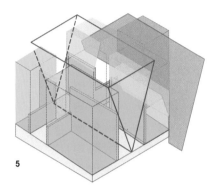

5

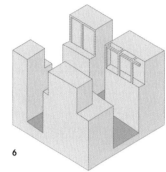

6

3-D rendering of Argent master-plan proposal with King's Cross and St. Pancras stations in foreground, looking north, 2007.

Excerpt from Argent Design Proposal "The Public Realm: A Walk through King's Cross Central" The public realm is at the heart of King's Cross Central. As a guiding principle it should connect real places together, integrate communities and their neighborhoods, and make the city safe to use and easy to understand. It would take about fifteen minutes to walk at a leisurely pace from Euston Road at the south end of the site to the top of York Way in the north. The site is divided naturally into three areas, each with a distinct character and would be held together by a network of routes and spaces which interconnect and link to the surrounding areas. The public realm at King's Cross Central would be a great 'breathing space' inserted among dense urban blocks and helping to bind them together. Its character, a combination of hard and soft, immense and intimate, historic and contemporary, would evolve from the site's topography, helping to steer the development towards a coherent and connected whole. Public spaces in and around King's Cross Central will be full of surprises: changes in level, broad vistas, glimpsed views; together creating the richness and drama which comes from embedding the new city into the old. It would combine busy places, calm places, places for strolling, sitting or sleeping in the sun. It would be the focus of life in this newly created district of London.

The Regent's Canal, with Granary Square at its center, would be at the heart of the public realm. This location was the hub of the site historically and would be reinvented as the meeting place of all major routes within the framework of King's Cross Central and of connections beyond the development proper. What was formerly a primary node for goods would now be a destination for people across London. It was and would be again a hive of activity, a market place, a place of business, competition and enterprise at the confluence of historic and contemporary transport routes. Collectively, the existing buildings at the center of the site establish its strong character. It would combine the toughness of the nineteenth century industrial landscape with the openness and buzz of new public spaces. Regent's Canal and Granary Square would not be a single space but a collection of public places split between two levels; the upper level of day to day and public life, and the lower level of the canal and Coal Drops Yard, devoted more to leisure, shopping and relaxation. It would combine the scale and history of well known London sites such as St. Katherine's Dock or the West India Quay with the intimacy and vitality of Camden Lock. This combination of busy urban space at the center of King's Cross Central and of softer, quieter places within the site would give the development a unique identity and would be the root of its enduring popularity and success.

The Boulevard, with Pancras Square, and the space of Long Park would allow the life and character of the Regent's Canal and Granary Square to permeate into all areas of the new development to south and north. Together they would form a central armature of connection across the site. The splaying shape of each space and the use of inflected geometries, especially at the point where the Boulevard meets Regent's Canal, would ensure continuity and flow for people moving through the site.

The context of the south section of the site is dominated by King's Cross and St. Pancras Stations with their long facades, robust architecture, and heavy passenger flow. The Boulevard and Pancras Square would together form a focus of the south, fanning northwards with two new routes and connecting across the Regent's Canal to Granary Square with two new bridges. At each end, Station Square and the Regent's Canal would form points of interlock, with Euston Road to the south and Granary Square to the north. As the site narrows to the south, existing buildings would be embedded within the new urban grain, while new structures, some free standing and some terraced, would be suitable for large floor plate office use, with a full range of retail and other public uses at ground level. The streets and spaces here would be interface and relate to London's large scale urban spaces such as Regent Street or Bishopsgate, with the exception that at King's Cross Central the pedestrian would have priority over most of the ground surface. The development would combine the coherent urban grain of parts of London such as Fitzrovia with the scale of Broadgate. A strong sense of urban enclosure would work with north-south permeability to give a dynamic but comfortable environment.

The north section of King's Cross Central would be larger and distinct from the south. Its central place, Long Park, would connect laterally and at its top end to York Way. Together with Granary Square and the Boulevard, it would form the backbone of the development, joining up to the site and connecting to its context. The urban grain of the north section of the site fans out to the south to meet the Regent's Canal, just as the railways did in the past. New blocks will interlock with

Aerial plan of Argent proposal for King's Cross Central, surrounded by central London.

existing historic structures to form an integrated piece of city. Every main street in the north section would have a mix of residential, office and other uses along it and would be active day and night. On the east side, York Way would form an active and permeable connector to neighboring areas. One part of the site, the Triangle Site, sits on the east side of the realigned York Way.

The developmental framework of King's Cross Central centers around a network of high quality public spaces. Development within this framework is scaled to permit a wide variety of use and building type, and allows uses and buildings to change and adapt incrementally against the background of a stable, inclusive public realm. This realization and acceptance that the city is a living and growing entity increases diversity, prolongs and enhances the lives of buildings, and would contribute to a long lasting city quarter which is socially and ultimately environmentally sustainable.

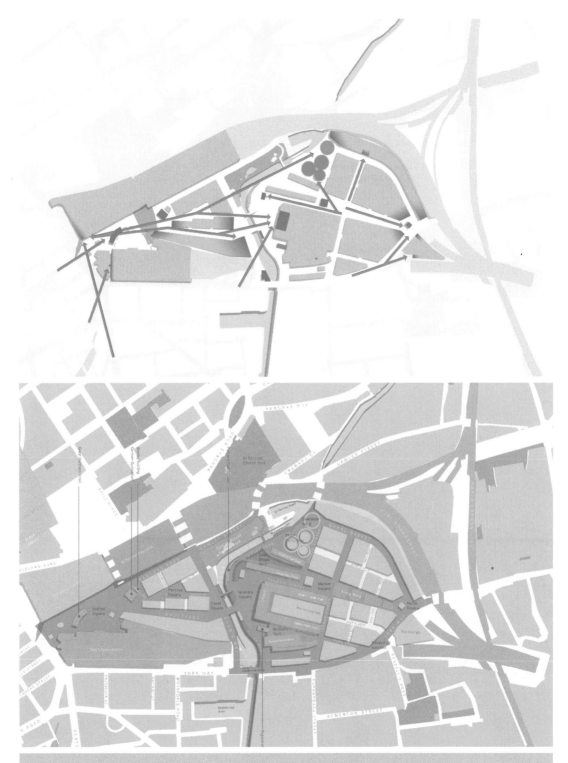

top: Site plan of King's Cross Central showing physical and visual urban connectors. bottom: Site plan of King's Cross Central showing framework for development as balanced between public space and buildings, with neighborhood spaces and private structures.

3-D rendering photomontage of Argent's Granary Square proposal from York Way. A generous space at the heart of the site serves as a place for formal events or spontaneous activity, as well as a focus for the life of King's Cross Central.

STUDIO
PLANNING

Site Analysis King's Cross Central presents an opportunity to shape a vibrant new urban quarter, held together by an architecturally coherent public realm. By creating connections within and beyond the site, establishing a robust urban grain and flexible mix of uses, reusing historic structures within a new framework, and maximizing the use of brownfields in this formerly industrial site, King's Cross Central will be a model for a sustainable piece of the city with a unique sense of place.

King's Cross St. Pancras is the only London Underground station served by six lines, and it is the third-busiest terminal in London. In addition, the proximity of King's Cross / St. Pancras to Euston Station—the terminus of major rail lines to north and west England—places King's Cross Central within easy reach of the Midlands, Scotland, and Wales. In 2007 the Eurostar Rail arrived at St. Pancras to connect the site to Paris, Lille, and Brussels, transforming King's Cross Central into an international hub and gateway to the U.K.

The site of King's Cross Central, previously known as the Railway Lands, and its potential have been trapped by railway infrastructure for 150 years. With the construction of the Channel Tunnel Rail Link into St. Pancras Station, this previously blighted site is being unlocked. Despite being centrally located in London, King's Cross Central is one of the economically deprived corners of both the Camden Town and Islington neighborhoods and is in need of large-scale regeneration.

The studio of the Edward P. Bass Distinguished Visiting Architecture Fellowship studied the master plan commissioned by Argent Group PLC and executed by a joint venture of Porphyrios Associates and Allies & Morrison as a tool to evaluate the relationships among the existing site's infrastructure, history, and proximity to the surrounding city and assess the potential of King's Cross Central to interconnect and enhance the city. The students investigated the relationship of historic structures to proposed development, various block and megablock massing strategies, existing and proposed green spaces, transportation transfers, and areas of urban transition between London and King's Cross Central as initial research to support future studio design work.

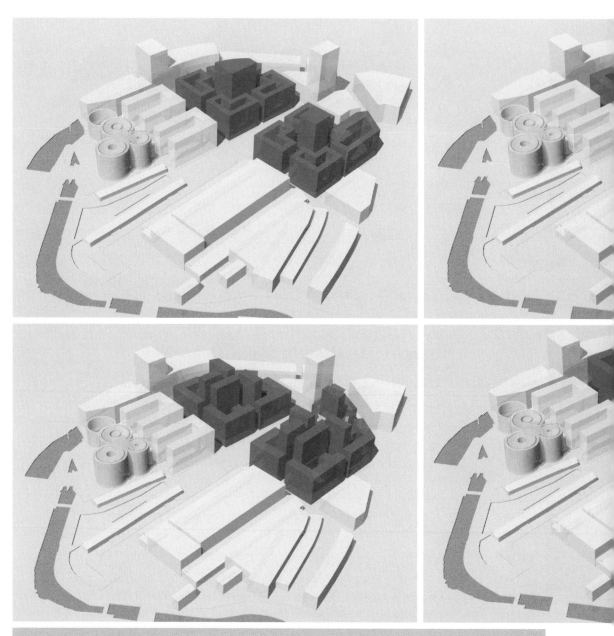

Megablock massing studies. top left: Perimeter courtyard blocks with central towers. top middle: Perimeter blocks with central stepped towers. top right: Perimeter blocks with multiple towers. bottom left: Perimeter blocks with slab high-rises. bottom middle: Tall perimeter blocks with low centers. bottom right: Variable-height perimeter blocks with low centers.

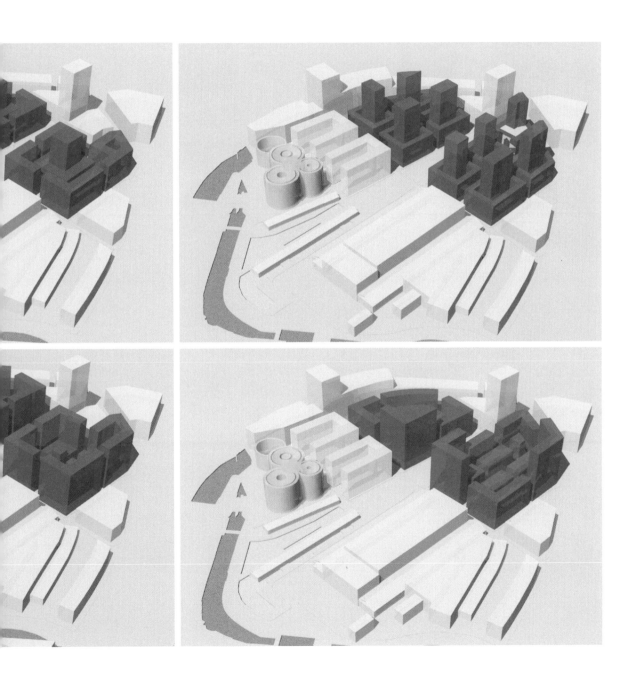

A comparison of the Railway Lands at the completion of the CTRL.

- **LINDSAY WEISS** BOULEVARD PREAMBLE
- **MAKO MAENO** MODERN TERRACE
- **KHAI FUNG** LIVE/WORK
- **SEUNG HWAN NAMGOONG** BRICK REVISITED
- **SINI KAMPPARI** HOTEL AND SISTER OFFICE BUILDINGS
- **ROSE EVANS** REGENT'S CANAL TOWER
- **AARON TAYLOR** TOWER AND VIADUCT
- **NEIL SONDGEROTH** THE TRIANGLE SITE

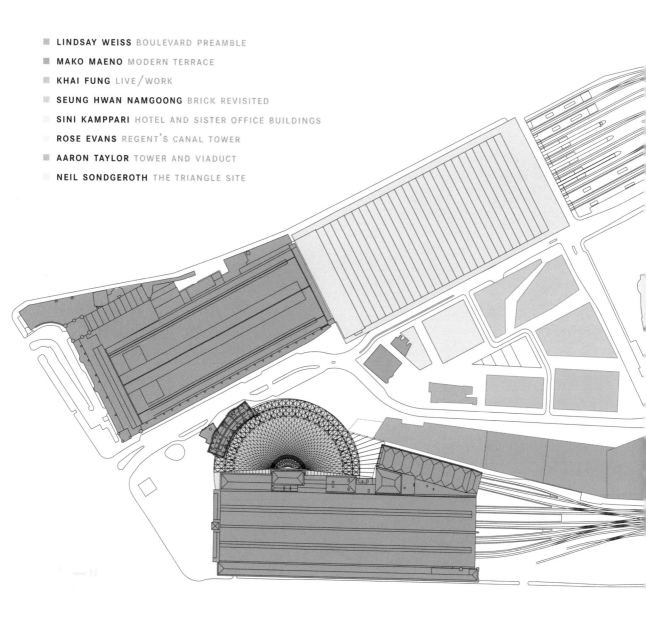

Expected development of the new King's Cross Central. Individual student projects are shown in separate colors.

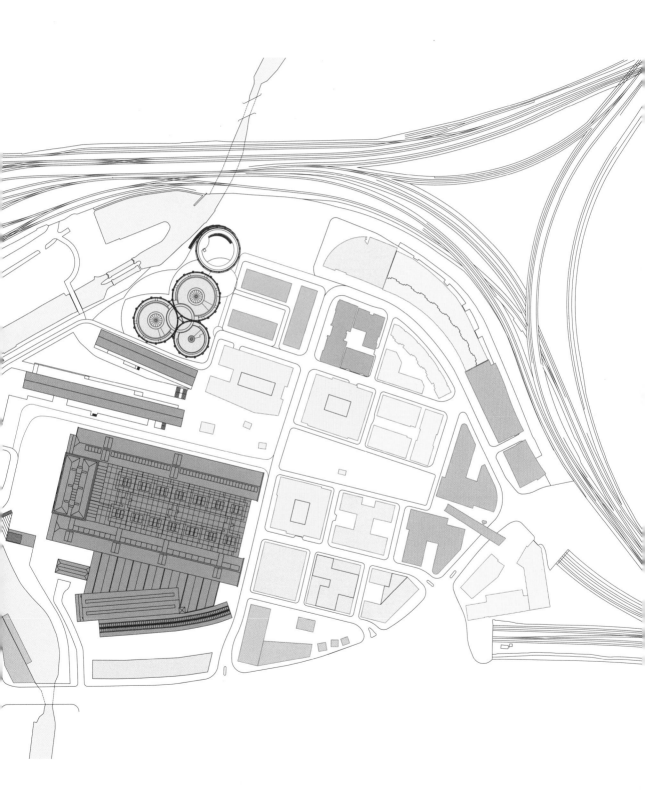

URAL

The first half of the King's Cross Central studio was devoted to individual student explorations of the themes of architectural character and typology as exemplified in the concept of the Human City.

The students first designed buildings based on the proposed Porphyrios Associates/Allies & Morrison master plan, which set the stage for the subsequent urban design phase of the studio. This existing master plan gave the studio a vehicle for understanding how the site could be developed within the context and guidelines of the planning office of the City of London, while also helping to focus and identify specific areas of urban intensity to be developed in urban design during the second half of the studio. The investigations prompted a dialogue between students and critics as to the role of various architectural typologies in the development of character and place. The question of how these typologies—by themselves and together as codified in the master plan—could engender architectural character for the establishment of a culturally sustainable city became a point of transition into urban design concepts.

Students were asked to design three to four buildings around the site, focusing on those structures that had prominent urban positions within the master plan. Each site was analyzed with regard to the most appropriate programmatic use and typological expression, including programs for residential, commercial, and civic usage, as well as the typologies of the tower, linear block, perimeter block, courtyard, terrace, palazzo, and villa. Special attention was given to the relationship of architectural character to public space, as well as the connectivity of new proposals to the existing historic structures and the context of the site.

3-D rendering of cantilevered element, which attempts to create an emphatic presence in the fractured urban space of Station Square. Simultaneously, it marks the beginning of the Boulevard urban sequence, that leads into King's Cross Central.

Lindsay Weiss This project is located at the intersection of the existing Station Square, sandwiched in between King's Cross and St. Pancras stations, and the proposed Boulevard, which forms the urban introduction into King's Cross Central. The addition of a new concourse at King's Cross Central exacerbates the fragmented urban situation of Station Square. As the entrance to the Boulevard, this site must simultaneously create an emphatic presence in Station Square but also set the stage for a well-defined and vibrant pedestrian space on the Boulevard.

The site this predominantly commercial building occupies makes it the most visually present addition to the urban perimeter of Station Square. My proposal was designed to intensify the severity of the collision between the two urban spaces by elevating eight stories above the square a two-story, 35-meter-long cantilever containing a bar and restaurant. The views up, into, and out of these spaces are breathtaking.

This fragmented shard of the Station Square urban environment is held aloft by a masonry podium consisting of office and retail spaces. The abrupt juxtaposition of the sleek glass shard with the solid masonry base was intended to amplify the fundamentally fragmented nature of the entry to the Boulevard. However, the massing, materiality, and composition of the masonry-podium façade initiates a well-defined urban space through which the remainder of the Boulevard can develop. This deference to the pedestrian scale of the Boulevard is accentuated by the introduction of a continuous arcade that connects directly to subsequent student proposals for the whole of the Boulevard space.

Façade model of the Cleft Building. The split composition of the façade articulates the fractured nature of Station Square as the building deflects pedestrian flow to the right down the Boulevard or to the left into Pancras Square. The "seismic" rupture line of the façade also serves as a visual indicator of the entrance to the Underground. opposite page: Aerial cutaway perspective.

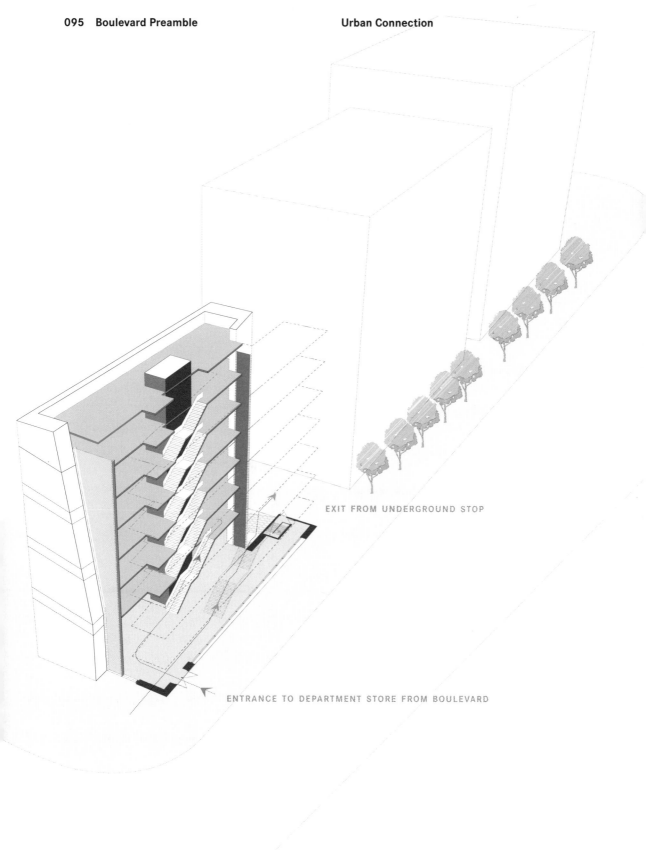

EXIT FROM UNDERGROUND STOP

ENTRANCE TO DEPARTMENT STORE FROM BOULEVARD

Discussion Roger Madelin: This project in experimental retail would make the Prada store in SoHo look old hat.

Jaque Robertson: Instead of making a cantilever that looks like it's made of mystery material, you actually take the plunge and do something tectonic. You're saying, "I know that Arup could make it stand up." But wouldn't the exciting thing be to show that the beak was articulated in metal, referring to both the past life of the gasometer and the future, at this most prominent point in the master plan? The enormous cantilever is so different from anything else on the building, so it is being expressed differently than the applied pieces. It is dramatic and perceptually powerful, but it is not architectonic enough. It makes an extraordinary space underneath it. The cantilever really has nothing to do with the base. I would have loved to have seen that whole piece in the back with a different kind of spatial aspect. Something like the gasometer aesthetic would have been quite striking, as the wonderful thing about this site is the collision of trains, gasholders, warehouses, and granaries.

Robert Stern: The problem is not whether it could be an icon, but that it is not iconic enough.

Jaque Robertson: It is a fabulous opportunity to work in the context of the genius of the nineteenth-century industrial vernacular on this site.

Robert Stern: In terms of the formal problems this building raises, I have always felt that a glass building jumping out the top of a stone building is a real problem. The other problem is the elevation is in the same plane as the other façades, but it's actually not in the same plane.

Tom Beeby: It has to do with the language of the building. There is a pseudo-structural language on the outside that does not correspond to the real structural language on the inside. I agree with Jaque on the power of the cantilever move, but the problem for me is the language is lacking in terms of a transition zone between the iconic cantilever and the base that forms the street edge.

Vincent Scully: You are right to make the great gesture at this point in the site, but you also felt the need to make a solid city wall to define the space below. This is a great struggle and an interesting point of transition because of these competing needs, the one static, the other active.

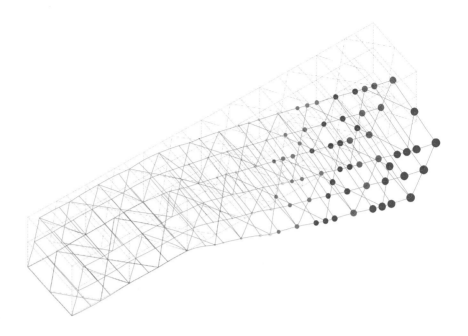

top: Structural diagram of cantilevered element produced in collaboration with Richard Henley, engineer at ARUP. bottom: Model of Boulevard Preamble Building cantilever showing base, office block, and glass atrium.

Study models of Boulevard Preamble and Cleft buildings.

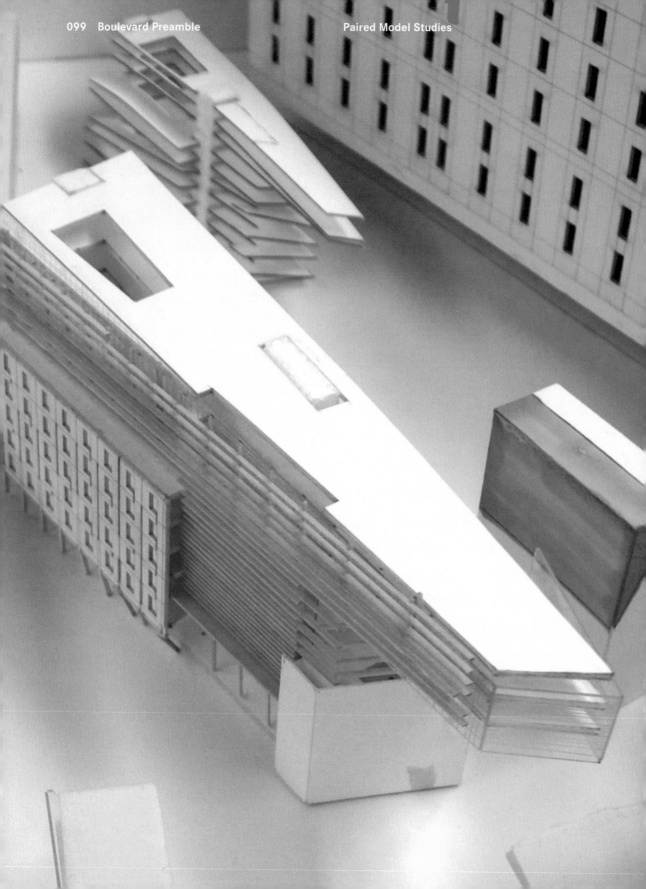

Model photomontage of the end condition of the Modern Terrace block illustrating the juxtaposition of urban (tower right) and industrial building (left) façade compositions as they address the exigencies of the site.

Mako Maeno Three buildings located along the Boulevard and railway leading toward King's Cross Station were contiguous and adjacent to Lindsay Weiss's "Boulevard Preamble" project, making the character of these buildings about creating two faces: one gesturing toward the railway and London, the other addressing the Boulevard and its lively pedestrian and commercial activity.

The two major façades of the Modern Terrace each have a different articulation and scale, reflecting the competing urban demands placed upon the buildings by the site. The railway-side façade is meant to be a massive curtain wall tying the three buildings together, thus attaining a large-scale elevation easily experienced from the moving train cars as they arrive at the station. Conversely, the Boulevard-side façade relates to the movement of pedestrians along the street. This is manifested in the decision to design three distinct façades that present themselves in syncopated succession, as shoppers, office workers, and residents experience the urban life of the Boulevard. Finally, the terrace and upper-floor plan contain atria in the first two buildings that open onto common roof terraces. This results in a continuous setback along the top edge of the Boulevard that reduces the overall height of the street wall and improves daylight levels for pedestrians.

For a typical floor plan, we capitalized on the slight deviation from the typical A-B-A visual cadence of a Renaissance elevation of the footprint in the second building and used optimum spans of fifteen meters to make an open office plan. The collision of the second building with the third and final building on the Boulevard creates unique conditions. We designed a small trapezoidal balcony along the Boulevard, and on the train side the shift in the floor plan produces the opportunity for more cellular spaces such as conference rooms, offices, and lounges emphasized by two rows of structural fins. The setback and arcade unifies the three buildings at the ground floor with the adjacent cantilevered structure.

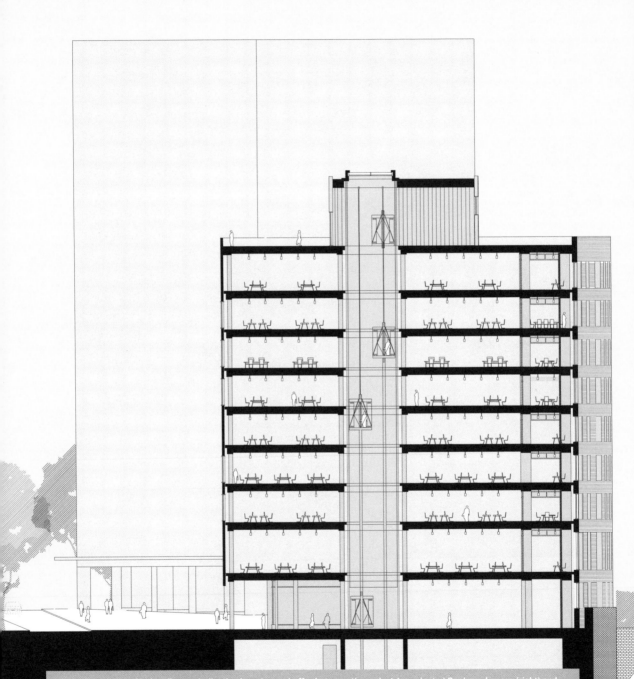

Section through the Modern Terrace indicating its role as a buffer between the pedestrian-oriented Boulevard space (right) and the industrial infrastructural space (left). The final segment of the Modern Terrace angles to serve as a visual indicator of the end of the Boulevard as well as to guide the viewer's eye toward Granary Square beyond. opposite page top: Exploded axonometric of the terrace showing ground-level, typical-level, and terrace-level floor plates. opposite page bottom: Study models investigating the articulation of the Terrace as it terminates the Boulevard, illustrating height and angle relationships between the principle street façade and the terminal end condition.

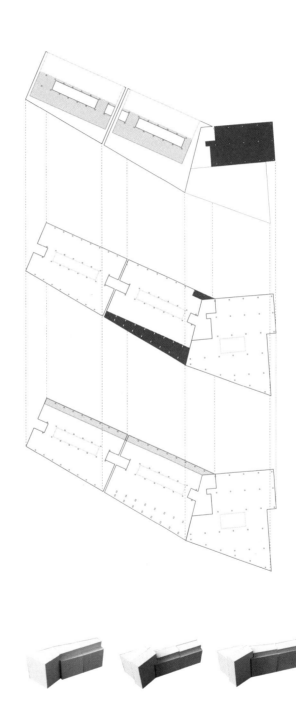

Discussion Jaque Robertson: In office buildings there are two or three really dumb rules; this may just be an exercise in punched windows that look good in certain proportions. There is a row of conference rooms that don't need much light and are somewhat cellular.

Tom Beeby: Normally the architect would not designate plans in the manner in which you are doing here, as the interior layouts would be variable so that the tenant who leases the space has the option of making his layout the way he wants, which makes the limitation of usage in this scheme problematic.

Graham Morrison: I think you need to avoid fashion. Every façade in London right now seems to be bar codelike elevations, which are just random vertical elements.

Alan Plattus: The wonderful thing about this scheme is the ambiguity between a piece of the street façade, to be composed of multiple buildings, and something that is supposed to be just one enormous extruded and attenuated building in its own right. If you can play up the ambiguity, then there is a real pleasure in what you are doing.

Demetri Porphyrios: If your scheme describes a terrace, then it will have a sense of scale. However, if the whole block were a megastructure, you would end up with an extremely large building. I agree with Tom that it should be continuous if there could be a language able to modulate itself significantly. But today we have no tools to design such long buildings other than those of a modern articulation. However, modern devices of articulation lack a sense of scale and character, which is why I feel that four or five buildings should be given to different architects who are sympathetic to each other so that they establish a dialogue.

Tom Beeby: I'm not so pessimistic. I think if you push in the right direction, you could get a more sophisticated modern architectural language. There were sophisticated façades during the Modernist movement, for instance, in Italy in the 1930s.

Vincent Scully: It is not a problem historically; it is a problem right now.

Model of the office building component of the live/work tandem.

Khai Fung This project consists of sites in both the southern and northern parcels of King's Cross Central on opposing banks of Regent's Canal. Since the master plan stipulated the southern parcel must be primarily office space and the northern parcel primarily residential, I designed my project around the idea of a micro urban "Live/Work" scenario. By framing the two sites in this manner I could compare and contrast the ways in which different urban typologies and façade strategies are employed within a visually concise urban environment.

The southern site is located at the center of Regent's Canal and faces directly opposite the historic Granary Building. Due to this disposition, my design breaks the nominal line of façades along Regent's Canal in order to address the public space of Granary Square. In addition, I proposed a small piazza as a way to connect visually to and extend the space of Granary Square. In creating this piazza I invoked the palazzo as an appropriate typology for the formality and frontality of this urban situation. Consequently, the design of the elevation was envisioned as a sparse Miesian grid, which reflects and defers to the historic masonry façades on the opposite banks of Regent's Canal.

The northern site is adjacent to Regent's Canal and near the new location of the historic gasholder structures. These gasholders, due to their unusual form and structure, as well as the manner in which they have been situated in a parklike setting, evoke an urban folly. To engage this situation, I designed for the residential building a U-shaped courtyard, which opens outward to embrace the vista of the gasholders. As a counterbalance to the urban palazzo type proposed for the southern site, I chose a pastoral villa type for this bucolic setting. This informal and residential atmosphere is further enhanced by the design of the façade wherein the fenestration of each unit varies according to its layout, resulting in a playful exterior appropriate to the relaxed character of the urban space.

Discussion Alan Plattus: When you look at the individual buildings all together, one could ask, Why do buildings next to each other facing the same street, or across from each other on the same street, have such dramatically different proportions of glazing to solid?

Tom Beeby: The master plan calls for a street on one side of your building and a square on the other. What obligation is there for the individual building designs to honor the street and square versus the object quality of their own formal process? In other words, what is the obligation of the Boulevard façade to the space of the street versus the plaza façade to the space of the square? Or is it all object-oriented, with alternating designs of the different façades?

Vincent Scully: One problem that really strikes me is scale. These structures are all screaming for a common language, regardless of whether it is Mies or Wren.

Alan Plattus: Would these elevations be any different if the floors were higher or three bays wider? It's so abstract that I am having trouble with the scale from the street level. There are many lan-guages that can help you with this, both modern and traditional, but you have to commit to the idea of scale.

Jaque Robertson: It could be done by Mies with the same curtain wall all the way around the building, with a corner articulation in a detail that would help with scale issues.

Ben Bolgar: Regarding the notion of public and private realms, the traditional urban block developed over millennia is based on particular ideas of size and permeability. What is the servicing strategy of the building? When a building is a whole block, each façade has an important urban space to address. How does it maintain this functionality, and why do you need to have such a permeable master plan?

Tom Beeby: There is a curious miniaturization that confuses how big these buildings really are.

Jaque Robertson: We do not possess a bird's-eye view but see the world from the ground. These drawings become misleading when we only discuss them from above without going down to the ground level.

OFFICE ENTRY
AND LARGE ATRIUM

RESTAURANT AND CAFÉ

Perspective cutaway 3-D rendering of office building showing atrium, office entry, and café restaurant. The prominent location of this building in the master plan requires the division of the ground level into public café space facing Regent's Canal and semi-private office-lobby space facing Pancras Square.

Robert Stern: When Mies designed the Seagram Building he only asked for two things: the building regulations of the city of New York and a model of Park Avenue made at his eye level. He studied that endlessly.

Jaque Robertson: The Seagram Building relates so beautifully to the Racquet Club across the avenue, and it results from Mies's perceptual attention. Seagram is the high watermark of a replicable skin. In fact, this whole block could be like that, but you have to see it from the ground.

Paul Finch: The relationship of public space to the buildings is interesting because the architectural exercise is asking some quite serious questions of the master plan, as they should in this type of setting. When someone comes along and actually makes a proposal for a piece of architecture and—guess what—it doesn't work with the spaces it is being put in, it might be the urban spaces that are the problem.

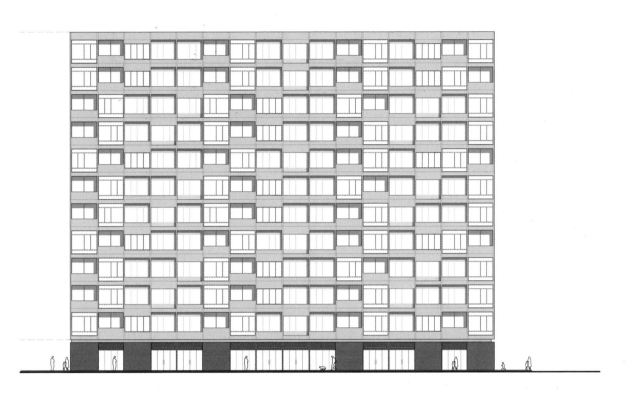

L LIVING
K KITCHEN
S STUDIO
B BEDROOM 1
B BEDROOM 2

Façade (top) and panel diagram (bottom) of Goods Way elevation. The panel location and fenestration reflects the layout of the unit types beyond, creating a pattern which enlivens the rectilinear massing.

3-D rendering of a brick-façade study showing the placement and variation of brick-corbelled bays between structural piers.

Seung Hwan Namgoong King's Cross Central is unusual in the sense that there is not a bad site in the development. Every building is important and holds different responsibilities that add value to the entire development. Each face of a building is uniquely articulated in order to serve the public space it is fronting, but at the same time all the faces of a building share fundamental, identifiable qualities. These qualities comprise materials, scale, surface treatment, and structure. In order to achieve this idea of multiplicity-in-singularity, "Brick Revisited" borrows techniques used in photography, such as panning, blurring, motion, and stills, to allow for the creation of multiple narratives based on concrete architectural elements. Four different buildings on four different sites, which have different conditions in terms of their importance, usage, and relationship with the surrounding sites, were formulated using the above techniques.

An office tower "bookend" engages the public by creating a connection point through the building within the city, showing a connection to other buildings in the site through its massing and materials of glass, masonry, and metal.

An office tower, "keystone," holds the significant responsibility of maintaining various relationships within the existing architectural geometry of the site. It expresses its materiality, creating visual connections with the existing historic buildings on the site. The differentiation of brick treatment on either side of the building results in a dynamic visual experience.

A six-story boutique retail building with a restaurant sits along the canal. Due to its location at the intersection of Goods Way and the Regent's Canal, this building functions as a gateway into the development and makes specific urban connections to the surrounding city infrastructure while simultaneously acting as an invitation to the site. The continuation of the existing retaining brick wall with dynamic fenestration, which changes in its section along the canal, sets the basic tone of the building as a significant connection between the old and new buildings. The thick brick wall becomes the base for the transparent glass box which opens itself to the public along Goods Way. A public building with a community garden on the edge of York Street divides the site from the neighboring town and attempts to stitch the two parts of the city together. A simple but elegant precast-concrete façade, which opens and closes at the garden level, forms a dynamic building.

Model illustrating the variable character of the different façades. The historic Regent's Canal is addressed with brick to reflect its focus on the human scale, while a glass curtain wall faces the busy vehicular thoroughfare of York Street, enabling easy viewing from passing traffic.

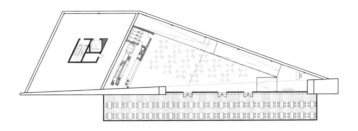

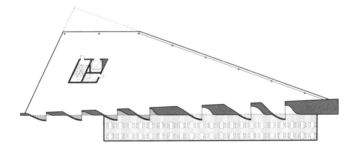

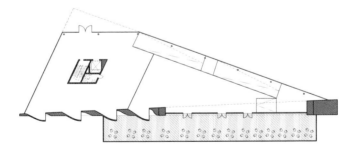

Café level (top), typical shop level (middle), and entry level (bottom). The café is located one level below the entry level to take advantage of the building's location along Regent's Canal. The generous arch opens the view from the café to vistas along the canal with opportunities for indoor/outdoor seating.

Discussion Roger Madelin: It's a new, smaller Guggenheim—a Guggenheim-lite.

Vincent Scully: A certain amount of unity suggests itself in this place, so I can see why one would want to make the gateway an ovoid shape. But then you've got the wonderful condition of the canal cut into the ground, and you can talk about real façades and real buildings, but you haven't responded to these conditions. These façades and your façade in particular must match up against the existing façades across the water.

Jaque Robertson: Bricks are tricky things that people have spent thousands of years playing with. Brick does certain things well and other things not so well. You can corbel them, true, but generally it's a pretty messy business. Mies's drawings are all done at full scale, helping him to understand the size of everything. Brick was one of his favorite measuring devices because you can hold it in your hand.

Tom Beeby: Yes, but Mies uses brick in a fairly conventional way. He wasn't wildly inventive with the way it is used structurally.

Paul Finch: In this part of London there are a lot of amazing Victorian brick structures. You can make brick do just about anything, if you understand its inherent qualities.

David Partridge: It's a fantastic scheme, but I hate to say it is on the wrong side of the canal. You've got a north face with the most fantastic views up the canal and the whole of King's Cross, and you close it up except for these small corbelled windows.

Graham Morrison: He is on the right side of the canal; he should just put the brick on the other side of the building.

Patrick Bellew: He should also have brick on the south façade for environmental reasons. Flipping the scheme around would solve this as well as what David is talking about in terms of views.

Roger Madelin: It is not an office or an apartment building, which would be dependent on the qualities of the view. It is Guggenheim-lite, and people are going to want to see what is inside of this idiosyncratic shape.

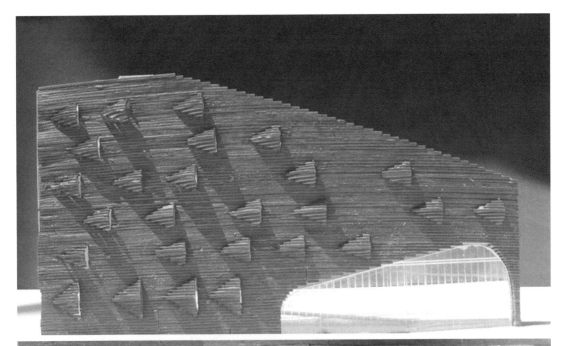

top: Diagram illustrating the development of the Regent's Canal façade and arch profile. middle: Model of Regent's Canal façade with ovoid arch leading to a café at the canal level and corbelled apertures offering a contemporary reflection of brick-bearing construction. bottom: Study model of corbelled brick apertures for the Regent's Canal façade.

Sini Kamppari The Sister Office Buildings are located at the intersection of Long Park and Goods Way, where the character of Long Park changes from a tree-lined park to a paved marketplace. Both buildings have towers that are slightly taller than the rest of the buildings and are visible from the southern part of the development, functioning as gateposts for the Long Park neighborhood of King's Cross Central. The general massing of each office building allows light to penetrate into the interior courts of the city blocks, of which they are a part.

Both buildings have retail uses on the ground level, especially on Goods Way. The main entry for each of the offices is located on Long Park. The generic floor plan aims to be as economical as possible but still includes a large central atrium that provides air and light. Indeed, the study of nominal typologies, in this case that of the office block, was one of the principal foci of the studio.

The rhythm of windows and partitions, as well as the choice of exterior materials, creates the building's character. The main towers are limestone with punched windows, whereas the rest of the building is a composite of Cor-ten steel fins, with wood and fritted glass panels in between. The Cor-ten steel fins refer to the steel of the railroad tracks previously located at the northern end of the site. A solid band of harvested wood located above the ground level establishes a visual distinction between the ground level and the top of the building.

The King's Cross Central Hotel faces a paved marketplace and is located between the historic Coal Drops Building and one of the Sister Office Buildings. Due to its location at the transition from the lower historic buildings to the taller structures of Long Park and Goods Way, the hotel has a lower massing and highly articulated ground floor. These features relate to the scale and character of the market as opposed to the quieter, tree-lined park, straddled by office buildings.

The overall massing of the building is very simple: two bays of hotel rooms flank an atrium. The chiseled face of the massing, as well as the whimsical pattern of the windows on the elevation,

opposite page: Elevation study model of the hotel illustrating the change in character of the façade between 3pm (top), 6pm (middle), and 9pm (bottom).

demonstrates the building's special character in relation to the marketplace. There are two entries into the hotel, one from Goods Way, with a taxi drop-off, and the other facing the marketplace. An arcade at ground level is in line with the historic Coal Drops Building and projects into the marketplace, providing a balcony at the third level of the building.

A significant lighting accent is given to the ground level at the entryway, as well as at the roof level with the hotel pool and roof deck. During the day, the mass of the building is prominent, whereas at night it fades away, and the two main lighting accents illuminate and add ambience to the nightlife of the marketplace.

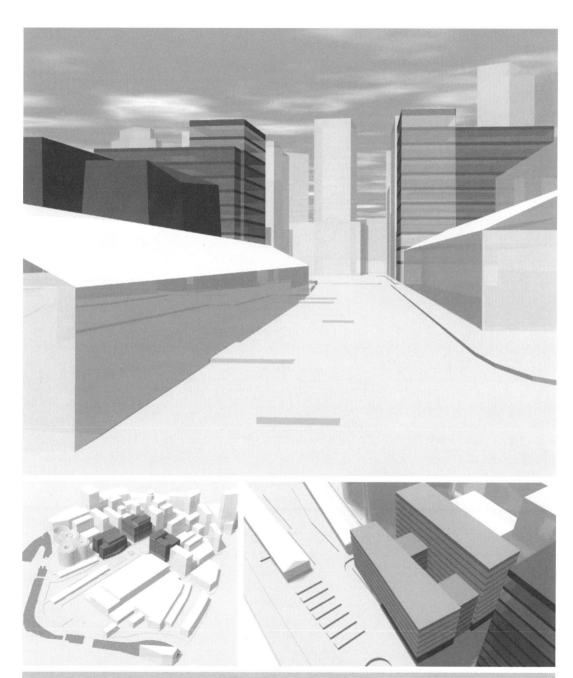

top: 3-D rendering of view from the corner of Granary Square down Long Park. The Sister Office buildings receive the visual thrust of the historic Coal Drops and Granary Shed as well as frame the proposed terminal tower of Long Park. The new hotel relates in height to the Granary across from it and serves to balance the composition by matching new and old construction in a dialogue of masses. bottom left: 3-D rendered aerial view of the north sector of King's Cross Central featuring the location of the hotel and Sister Office Buildings at an important crossroads of the site. bottom right: 3-D rendered aerial view of the hotel. The massing strategy of parallel bars is inspired by the bar typology of the historic Coal Drops Building, while the height of the bars steps down toward the public space in an effort to ease the height transition between historic and new construction.

Discussion Demetri Porphyrios: This is a very inventive and successful scheme. What you propose is quite significant: you bring the line of the Coal Drops Building into the public space. It is very clear as a composition that works as a grouping of masses and as an urban space.

Jaque Robertson: You could also play with the awning—it could be curvilinear or faceted—and the directionality of the grain and the kink are the right moves at the end of this space. It is a very simple but powerful idea that could be very nice. The moves you make with the hotel lead the eye to the pairing of the office buildings. It is interesting how a drawing tells us the height and angle are right. This is the power of a good drawing. The twin façades are interesting for their modernist, stripped-down, almost pre-Rossi-esque sensibility, which actually could go either way—either as modernist or traditional buildings—so they are a kind of swing façade.

Alan Plattus: I appreciate the effort you and the group have made toward some sort of common façade articulation. Here we have an especially clear relationship, given its position in the master plan. The fact that you've made them not quite the same is a little too inscrutable given the understood set of rules that you have given yourself. I understand the urban logic and its repercussions on the façades.

top: Cubitt Square façade elevation. bottom: Goods Street façade elevations.

Model of Regent's Canal Tower scheme.

Rose Evans Goods Street bisects the King's Cross Central development, bringing spaces for education, art, retail, offices, and dining to the heart of the new neighborhood. The terminus of Goods Street at the tracks of the new Eurostar station requires a statement at both the local and global scales. From the elevated Eurostar train, travelers experience their first glimpse of London as the train exits the tunnel and slows to a halt at the base of the proposed Regent Canal Tower's glazed curtain wall. The southern façade of the building is set back from the site perimeter to allow this view when the adjacent site is developed into "London's Greatest Pub."

Vehicular and pedestrian traffic arrives at the Regent Canal Tower's main entrance to reception areas alongside a large gallery and auditorium. The tower's entrance glows beneath a curved stone façade. A restaurant follows the south-façade curtain wall as it sweeps around to the front of the building. Floor plates vary throughout the tower to permit a variety of activity in the building's 40,000 square meters. Floors two through fifteen provide diverse rental opportunities, integrating the crescent-shaped tower and the spaces surrounding an atrium. Several floors above the atrium take advantage of panoramic views of London. The crescent rising into the sky includes 5,000-square-foot floor plates and accommodates luxury condominiums, boutique hotel suites, and small businesses interested in having a special office floor with private reception areas.

The tower respects views of St. Paul's Cathedral and the Palace of Westminster while supplying density and diversity of program pivotal to the life of Goods Street. The issue of the site's difficult back-of-house location is resolved by making the building's program as lively as possible, both by day and by night. Drawing in businesspeople, gallery- and event-goers, diners, residents, and hotel guests to the end of Goods Street ensures its vitality, while the tower serves as a representative beacon of King's Cross Central throughout London.

Regent's Canal Tower study model analyzing the transition from horizontal street element to vertical canal element.
opposite page: Sketches investigating the relationship between the curved tower form and its rectilinear base.

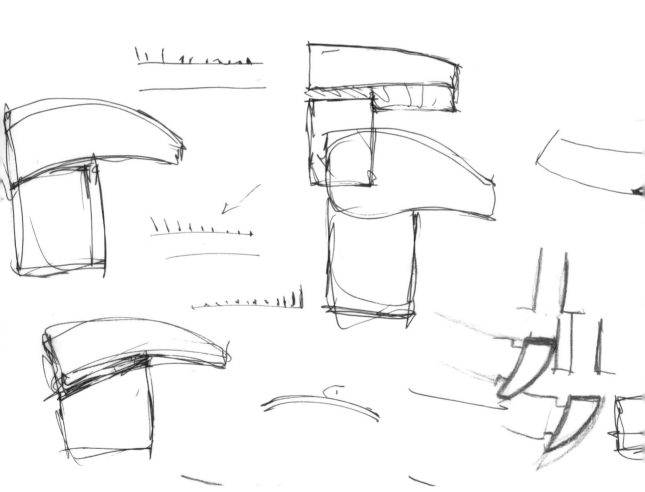

Discussion Peter Bishop: I am rather skeptical of some of those long-range views to St. Paul's and the view corridors from it, but I'm not skeptical of some of the mid-range and short-range views. I am interested to know whether you considered that to be an issue in choosing the site for this tower. The placement of the gasholders in the master plan was such that it created quite an interface between the old buildings and the new, which I think the tower would now alter quite radically.

Paul Finch: I think getting rid of the block in front of the tower works. It makes more of the end of that portion of the site available to the canal as public space as it bends away. Your tower actually marks that point of bending. I think the mix of uses in the tower is great. I think you need to signal the top of the tower as having some sort of public purpose, whether it is a restaurant or bar or whatever, so that it will be open all through the evening. Actually, you could put anything next to the gasholders, and it wouldn't make any difference. They are what they are, and they have their own strength.

David Partridge: We've seen a lot of elevations today, yet somehow composing them and thinking about them from the ground and in 3-D in relation to the buildings around them would give us a much better feel for what kind of place they make.

Jaque Robertson: These issues are almost constants throughout the history of architecture. The act of choosing precedents that you like for this or that reason and the analyzing of those reasons helps you a lot when you run into situations like this.

Demetri Porphyrios: I think the hotel is a good idea. I do worry though, since these buildings along the crescent act as a noise barrier to the trains. The sense of barrier and edge may be lost if you open it up along the tracks.

David Partridge: It is relatively close to the canal waterfront, which is the heart of the development at night with night clubs and cafés. I think that its height and location allows people to see it from the train stations.

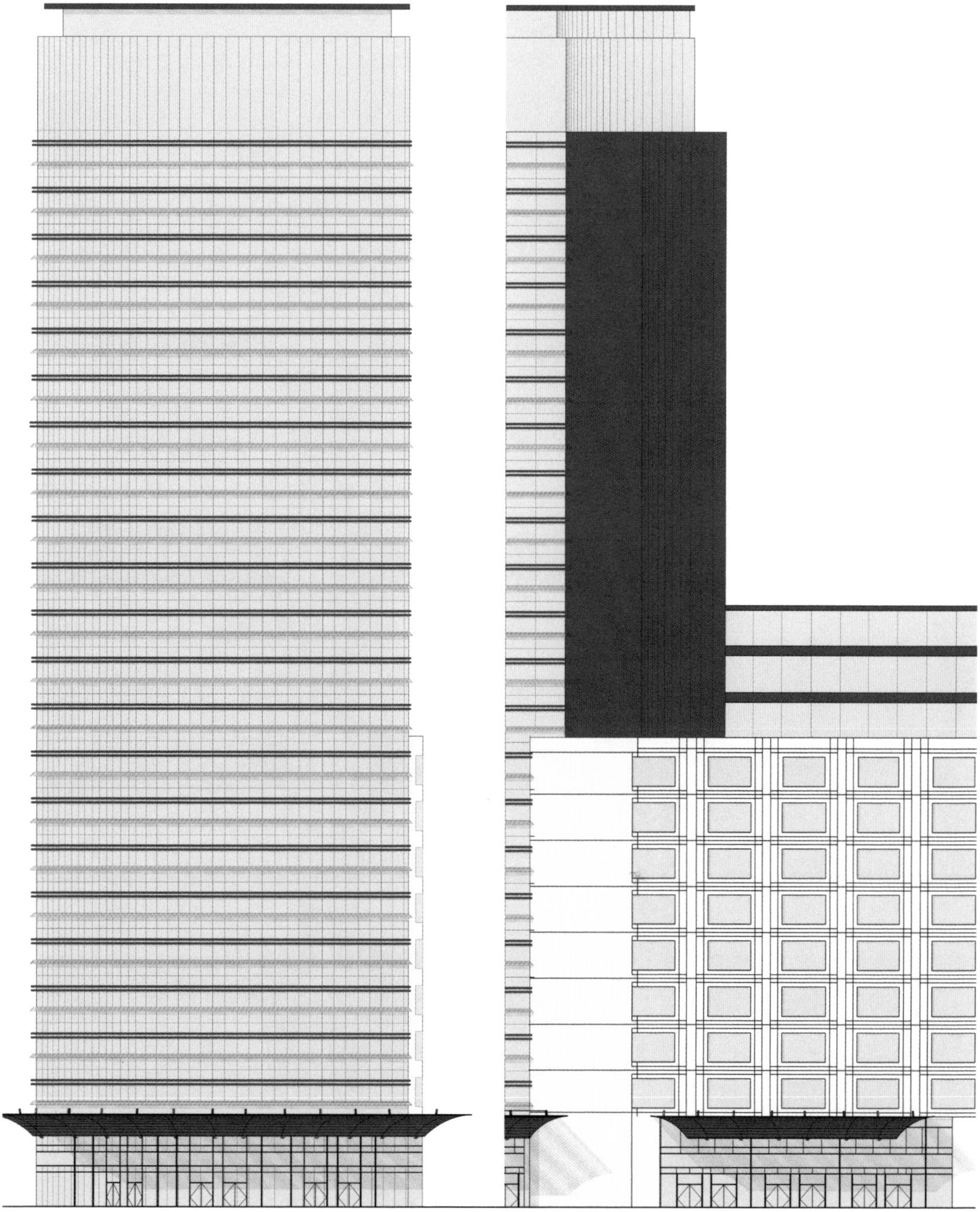

Elevations of Regent's Canal Tower Goods Street façade (left) and Canal Street façade (right).

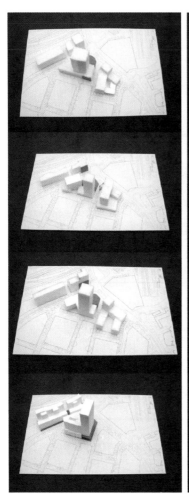
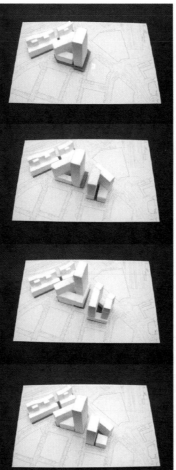
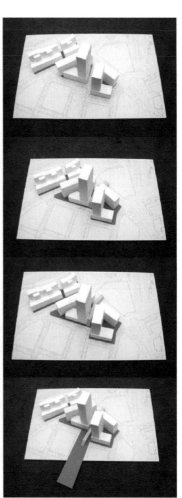

left to right: Massing study models of Tower and Viaduct scheme from initial findings, midterm, and final review.

Aaron Taylor The Tower Viaduct project makes use of vertical and horizontal urban elements to address various opportunities within the King's Cross Central site, which is the focal point of Long Park, located at the northern end of the Long Park neighborhood. A conscious effort was made to create a gateway at the end of the park in order to open the northern end of King's Cross Central to greater London.

Two five-story mixed-use podia are oriented so that they evoke a gateway into the park toward the interior of the scheme, while the opposite-facing courtyards provide resident access from intimate side streets. Each podium supports a multistory residential tower that further enhances the idea of an urban gateway to Long Park. The taller tower addresses the park frontally from the end axis of the urban space; the shorter tower is located to the side of the park and steps downward in height to relate visually to the façades that define the perimeter of Long Park.

Finally, a pedestrian bridge, the Viaduct, thrusts between the two vertical elements and connects directly to the plaza of an adjacent student site that was cut off from the master plan by the heavy traffic of York Way. This pedestrian bridge functions not only prosaically as a newly created urban artifact that invites the continuity of pedestrian flow across the site but also temporally, as it evokes the historic Victorian structures found across the site in both space and time.

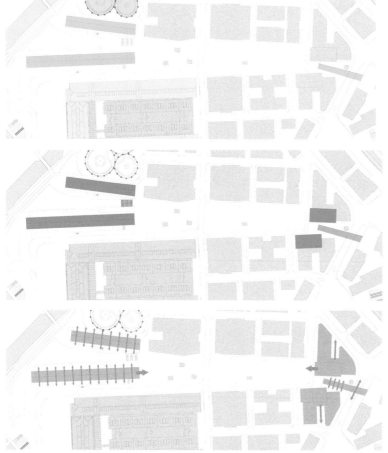

FIGURE/GROUND
EXISTING GRANARY AND
COAL DROP STRUCTURES WITH
PROPOSED YORK WAY VIADUCT.

SITE STRATEGY
EXISTING HORIZONTAL HERITAGE
STRUCTURES WITH PROPOSED
VERTICAL HOUSING TOWERS.

SITE FAÇADE ARTICULATION
FRONTAL-END FAÇADES ON LONG
PARK WITH POROUS-SIDE FAÇADES.

top: Site diagrams, opposite page: Study sketch perspective of tower from Long Park.

Discussion Tom Beeby: I like the fenestration and commend you on the way you differentiate the façade based on program distribution and varying conditions of gravity loads to make a much more evocative elevation, but it is still rudimentary. You show that you don't have to slap on a historical façade to arrive at a rational and evocative approach.

Robert Stern: You do have to get your client to support certain kinds of moves inside the building or else they will say the units are unmarketable. I might buy your argument about the windows and unit types, but you need to take the glass up all the way to the top of the tower.

Alan Plattus: The diagrams show there is an affiliation between the buildings your scheme proposes and the older infrastructure. Look to the gasholders as a reference for an exposed, skeletal aesthetic for the towers.

Demetri Porphyrios: There are two moves that are quite significant: The viaduct suggests a host of possibilities and resonates historically, while the organization of the two towers creates a gateway to Long Park, which acts in concert with Sini's Sister Office Building scheme.

Peter Bishop: There is something rather comforting as a Londoner about seeing that bridge as one travels down York Way. The idea is that there's a reminder of the older Victorian buildings in the south parcel, which is reflected in the set-piece Viaduct that helps to tie the north and the south parcels together.

Jaque Robertson: You saw the Coal Drops, you saw an old Ledoux book, and you said, "I can do something here that has a powerful presence." Here's the issue: the taller of the two towers has to be palpably different at the top. They can't be just two buildings where one stopped while the other kept growing. The elevations should be individually articulated.

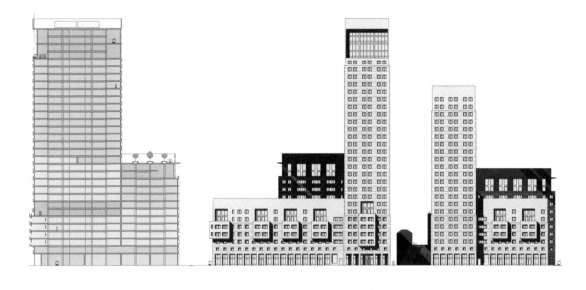

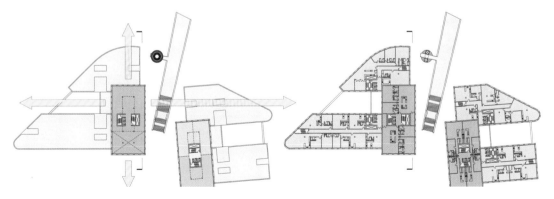

clockwise from top right: Tower and Viaduct Long Park elevation, ground-level plan, typical-level plan, and longitudinal section through the tower.

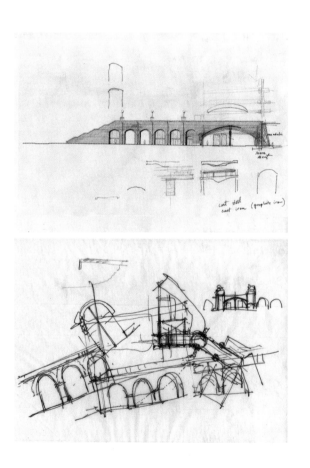

opposite top: Sketch façade study of York Way viaduct. opposite bottom: Study sketch of York Way viaduct. above: Detailed partial elevation and section of York Way viaduct. Students were encouraged to explore and reinterpret tectonic relationships of traditional building techniques.

3-D rendering of the Triangle Site from York Way.

Neil Sondgeroth The Triangle Site has few of the advantages of other blocks in King's Cross Central. It is isolated from the site by the busy thoroughfare of York Way, and it is deep to the center yet offers few viable frontages that would allow for architectural expression. Compounding all this is the significant change in grade elevation from the north of the site to the south. To deal with these issues, I developed a strategy that organized the development around two open spaces: one is a public plaza off the viaduct—proposed by Aaron Taylor—that terraces down to an adjacent interior courtyard. The interior is meant to be accessible to all three of the building masses on the site. The site features a residential tower that establishes a strong anchor point at the tip of York Way. The tower was designed to a height that is responsive to that of the adjacent student proposals at the end of Long Park. The second mass is lower and serves to shield the site from the rail lines immediately to the north. The mass is a gymnasium that provides a public function for the site and relates in scale to the housing developments to the east. The complex as a whole is meant to offer a sense of community within, yet at the same time serve as an extension to the whole of the Long Park.

Discussion Alan Plattus: The parking will help to sell the units because tenants can have their car in the basement garage. As an office building, this is a little remote from where the action is, but as housing it would work well.

David Partridge: The way this site was arranged in our scheme was that the tall tower was located in the middle, where your courtyard is. One of the reasons for that was to give views right down Long Park.

Demetri Porphyrios: As one approaches from the north, the site is very dense, and it doesn't feel like it was a place at all. The great terrace that you are proposing and the connection to the viaduct is both a clever solution and a complete urban composition. What makes the shift possible is that the viaduct comes all the way up to the base of your towers and it gives a pattern to the Triangle Site with a view all the way down Long Park.

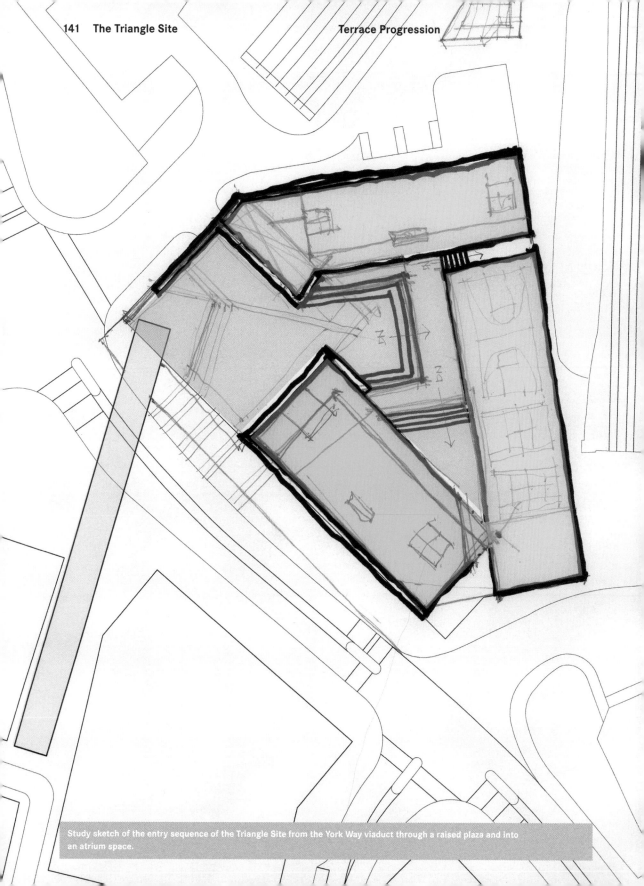

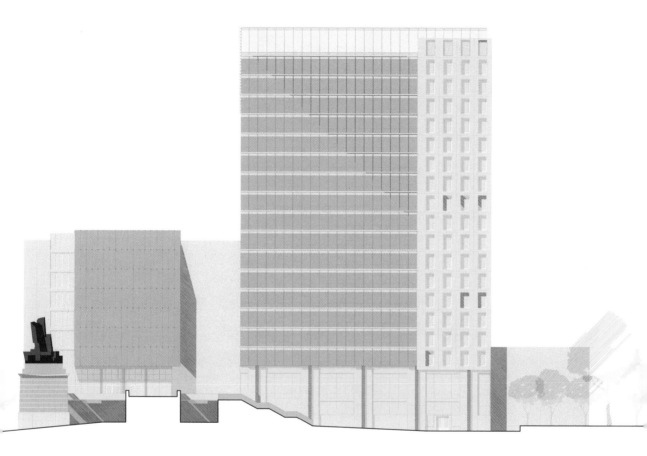

URBAN DESIGN

Design Studio, Phase Two The goal of the second half of the King's Cross Central studio was to bring the individual student designs into concert with one another in order to create coherent and meaningful urban spaces for this new district of London.

The primary lesson from the explorations from the first half of the studio revealed the need for a greater degree of conversation among the student designs. A lot had been achieved at this point, but there was little coordination among individual student projects on adjacent sites as to the character of the urban space as a whole.

The students took it upon themselves to organize into groups based on the neighborhoods surrounding the principal urban spaces of King's Cross Central. These urban districts were given names in order to help focus and refine the specific character of each space: the Boulevard, which connects to Station Square and the existing train stations in the south; Regent's Canal, with Granary Square as the heart of the development; Goods Street, the major vehicular connector, and Long Park, the breathing space at the northern half of the site. Each group subsequently identified prominent urban buildings within their individual neighborhoods and found ways for secondary buildings of each neighborhood to organize around these to form coherent places. This studio reorganization inspired discussions among the students and among the students and critics as to the nature of architectural relationships, the different levels of sympathy among individual designers, the degree to which a common set of principles can foster the development of character, and the value of architectural narrative as a paradigm for the creation of meaningful human environments.

Model of the Boulevard scheme.

Lindsay Weiss, Mako Maeno, and Khai Fung The addition of a new concourse to King's Cross Central will produce a leftover space, Station Square, between it and the adjacent St. Pancras Station. Our first task was to address this space with the goal of making it more regular and legible as the major access point to the development.

The main space that connects to Station Square, the Boulevard, is extremely different in character. The scale and activity along the Boulevard points to a vibrant pedestrian life, which is reinforced by a continuous arcade marking the route to the two stations. St. Pancras Square is flanked by buildings that perform as objects, where most of the commercial activity occurs. The four façades visible from Station Square demand an identity to entice users into the heart of the development.

The master plan has dictated a severe point of connection between the new concourse at King's Cross Central and the south side of the Boulevard; we have chosen to intensify this severity by elevating the southern tip of the building eight stories off the ground within a two-story, 35-meter cantilever containing a bar and restaurant.

Based upon the master plan, the length of the Boulevard was subdivided among three students. To ensure a level of continuity for the urban space of the street while allowing individual site development, we chose the traditional London terraced housing as the defining typological ideal. Following this choice we developed relative building heights and set-back criteria to foster a dialogue among separately evolved designs. Finally, we adopted a continuous street arcade along the length of the Boulevard to tie our proposals together at the pedestrian level.

The northern end of the Boulevard intersects the Regent's Canal and acts as a gateway to the northern side of King's Cross Central. The final site of the Boulevard cants outward both as a way to invite the flow of people into the Boulevard from Station Square as well as to direct the view of pedestrians toward the historic Granary Building across the Regent's Canal. Due to its special location and function along the Boulevard, the final building of our urban design was allowed to rise above the height level of the terrace typology and thus serve as a terminal vertical balance to the emphatic horizontal cantilever at the southern end of the street.

top: Composite student east-elevation drawing of the Boulevard. bottom: Composite student plan drawing of the Boulevard.

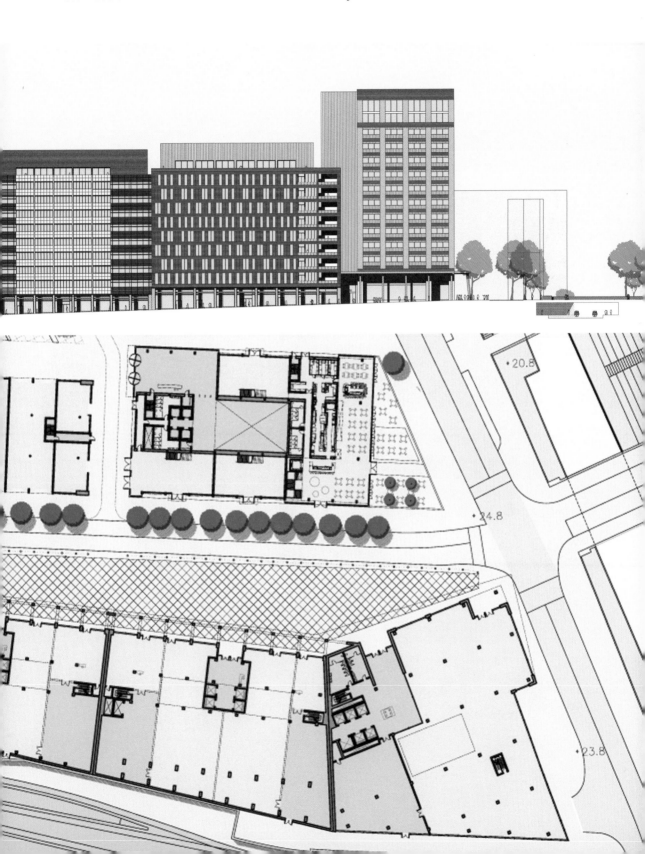

ZONE B

ZONE A

PANCRAS SQUARE

BOULEVARD

Aerial view of Station Square and the Boulevard. Three principle façades (orange) produce containment along the northern edge of Station Square while the stepped massing (yellow and tan) visually invites pedestrians into the Boulevard. The angled end of the Boulevard diverts the flow of traffic toward Granary Square.

Discussion Vincent Scully: You have a traditional plan that requires solid blocks defining voids, plazas, streets, and so on, but you design these blocks in a very modern idiom, which is reflective, transparent, and doesn't have the built-in movements from ground to top. So there seems to be a very basic struggle here.

Paul Finch: I think you have to admit you've been given a fantastically difficult task because it has automatically raised the question of the distinction between the ordinary and the extraordinary. You have two extraordinary pieces of architecture in King's Cross and St. Pancras stations. What you've been asked to do is to set up an urban route from an entrance hall to a grander piece of architecture, which is the station itself. The question is, are you competing with the Victorian train sheds and other historic buildings on the site? If so, then how far do you want to push it? Or are you saying the stars of the show are already there, and our task is to give meaning to the Boulevard. For me, it is a question of the hierarchy of the kind of extraordinary things that you've put on the site.

Graham Morrison: There are two things already asking questions of the master plan. The first is that to do something essentially aggressive at this end of the Boulevard in relation to the lack of coherency of Station Square is a good representation. Second, taking advantage of the extra height at the other end of the Boulevard and to point to the end piece this way is fantastic. What worries me is what is happening in between the two ends. What is the whole façade trying to say? I think there is a real issue about the impulse to start recomposing every building. How does the collaboration still establish a difference among individual buildings? As architects, you have to cope with doing extraordinary things but also doing things that are very ordinary and full of repetition.

Peter Bishop: We've focused on the Boulevard elevation up till now, and we haven't really talked about the back elevation. This side along the train tracks is what I think most Londoners will see of the development as they come in on the trains. It is an incredibly powerful element.

The Boulevard is envisioned as a thriving commercial street serving as the gateway into King's Cross Central. A pleasant mix of shops, restaurants, and offices provides the framework for multiple activities throughout the day.

Urban Rhythms

Regent's Canal urban collage captures the excitement and dynamism at the heart of King's Cross Central.

Khai Fung, Mako Maeno, and Seung Hwan Namgoong The location of King's Cross Central at the intersection of the historic infrastructural networks gives the site its character. Regent's Canal is the most intact piece of this infrastructure and the element around which much of King's Cross Central is planned.

Foremost among the canal's challenges and opportunities is the fact the canal bisects the master plan into north and south sectors. It was particularly important to our group to create a level of visual continuity and dialogue that would tie the two parcels of the site together. Second, the expanse of Regent's Canal and its planned use as a pedestrian thoroughfare presented us with the paradox of creating a new face for the city within the existing context of greater London. Finally, this new face of the southern part of King's Cross Central needed to address and relate to the historic industrial buildings on the opposite side of Regent's Canal.

Consistent architectural elements, appropriate scale, and materiality were the three major guiding principles we adopted in our search for an architectural character that would answer the challenges of the canal. The general height and scale of the buildings creates a compositionally balanced skyline. The buildings along this neighborhood use similar materials, such as glass, brick, and steel, to create a consistent and recognizable canal frontage but also to evoke many of the qualities found in the historic buildings. In this way we hoped to foster an architectural conversation between the past, present, and future of Regent's Canal.

top: Composite student east-elevation drawing of the Boulevard. bottom: Composite student plan drawing of Regent's Canal.

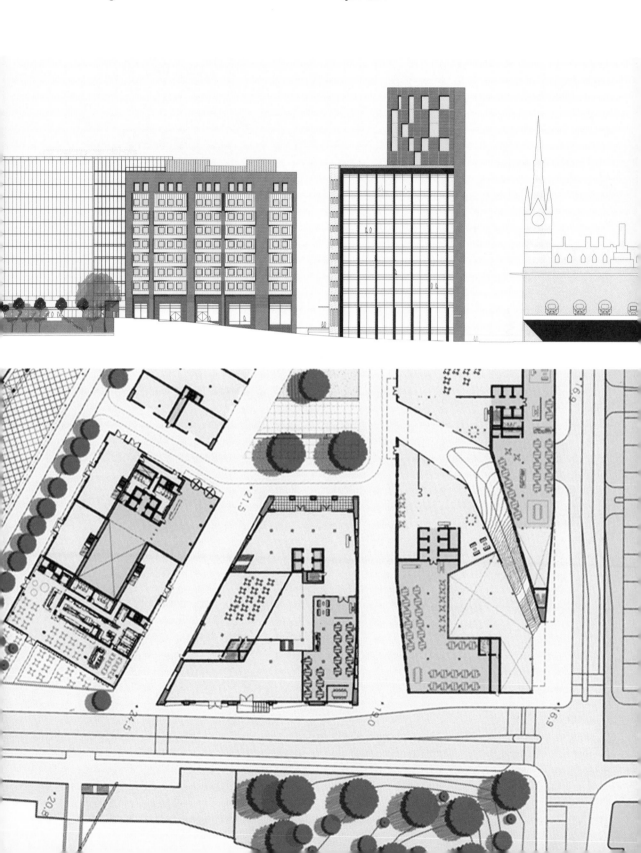

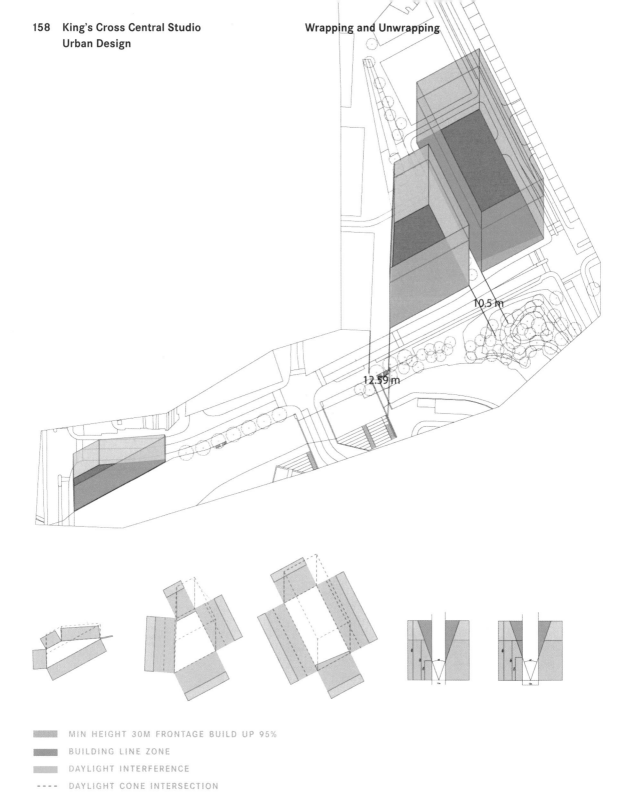

MIN HEIGHT 30M FRONTAGE BUILD UP 95%

BUILDING LINE ZONE

DAYLIGHT INTERFERENCE

---- DAYLIGHT CONE INTERSECTION

top: Axonometric study of Regent's Canal façade relationships. bottom: Axonometric diagrams showing façade height and set-back requirements.

Discussion Demetri Porphyrios: This is a long-distance view of the city from inside the city. Venice, Paris, Budapest, and a few other cities have the opportunity to do that as well. One would have liked all these buildings to read together as the face of the city by relating to each other while maintaining their individual character.

Graham Morrison: It is clear from the model that we all see different things when we see these renditions. These are huge, great façades, and one of the things I would certainly want to look for in terms of space-making is that they ought to produce an edge to the canal front. All the architectural interest is on the other side with the heritage buildings, except for the fact that the central building breaks the rule and is set back at an angle because of the inherited geometry of the south side. It produces an inflection that announces that particular position in the master plan, and this takes you back down to King's Cross. I think it would have been more powerful if all the façades had been different yet maintained some sort of consistency.

Peter Bishop: That raises the exact point that came up earlier: if everything becomes marginally different, then that jumble becomes relatively homogenous. You should have quieter, more related buildings. That is what is lacking in the scheme: everything is too different.

Jaque Robertson: Homogeneity is what you find in most great architectural cultures. I think this whole city façade requires that kind of joint action. Each place needs to look like it has some sort of quality of character rather than the attitude of "let me show you what I can do as a designer." Alan Plattus was talking about the Yale colleges and their fantastic variety from the hand of one or two architects. They developed their own language. Neo-gothic buildings at Yale are different than any others in the world, yet they use a common language upon which they can build. This district can have that quality if you don't try to do the zoo on each block. This opportunity in London is all about not doing another zoo.

Alan Plattus: It seems to me also that this is a place in the master plan where this whole section of façade could be a little more spirited and fun. There is a series of potential bases that have to do with the distance from the canal edge. Then there is another datum that I could imagine as a skyline.

Maybe from a common cornice height you let people do little follies on the roofs. A strategy such as this might accomplish both homogeneity and variety and would make a great advertisement for the rest of the city.

Robert Stern: I think that would be very interesting in London because there is not an especially interesting existing skyline.

Graham Morrison: One of the problems that we confront as master planners is, sometimes you have too much choice, and therefore every architect is tempted toward self-expression. This tends to generate difference rather than similarity. I think this is one of the things highlighted this morning.

Paul Finch: I think it is the ordinary against the extraordinary. Let's face it: that problem has essentially arisen because of speculative office buildings. The models for that are themselves multifarious, and what we are seeing now in London is a playing out of that on a very large scale. It is being played out in Dubai and Shanghai and everywhere else and in a very modest way here.

Model of Regent's Canal scheme.

Massing study of Goods Street seen from York Way.

Rose Evans, Sini Kamppari, Khai Fung, and Seung Hwan Namgoong Goods Street is one of the major thoroughfares connecting King's Cross Central to greater London. As such, it forms an east-west vehicular counterbalance to the primary north-south thrust of pedestrian flow.

Due to its function as a crossroads for the northern section of the site, Goods Street must address many points of urban connection. For instance, the street serves as an urban transition between the historic Granary and Coal Drops buildings located along Regent's Canal and the new development proposed for Long Park. In addition to this transition between old and new buildings, Goods Street is also an urban element that ties the older neighborhood of Islington to the new neighborhood of King's Cross Central. Finally, our group recognized that Goods Street must address the terminal condition of the street as it ends at Canal Street along the existing Eurostar rail lines.

Building massing, materiality, and modulation of the street section were our primary working themes so that the project could integrate with the existing context. For instance, in order to relate to the shorter heights and residential quality of Islington, we proposed a glazed-brick storefront community center and garden at the point of contact between the two neighborhoods at King's Cross Central. Similarly, a proposed stone-and-glass arcaded hotel picks up the horizontal massing, height, and plan geometry of the adjacent historic structures while directing the eye to taller, matching masonry office towers that frame the entrance to Long Park and the rest of the northern section of the site. As a solution both to make Goods Street an emphatic culmination and to give King's Cross Central a visual presence in the general context of London, we designed a sleek glass tower, which picks up on the sweep of the rails and the feeling of speed of the approaching Eurostar trains.

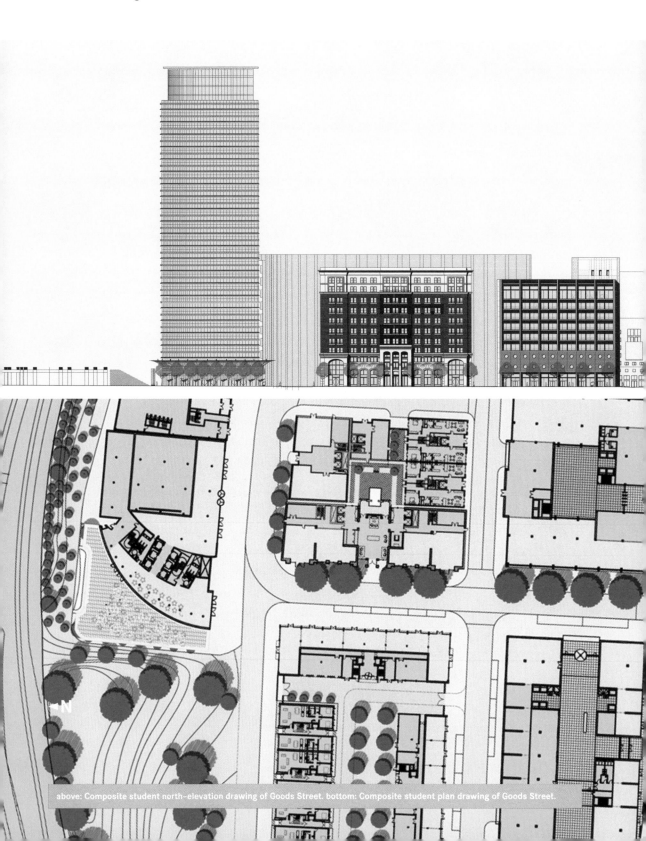

above: Composite student north-elevation drawing of Goods Street. bottom: Composite student plan drawing of Goods Street.

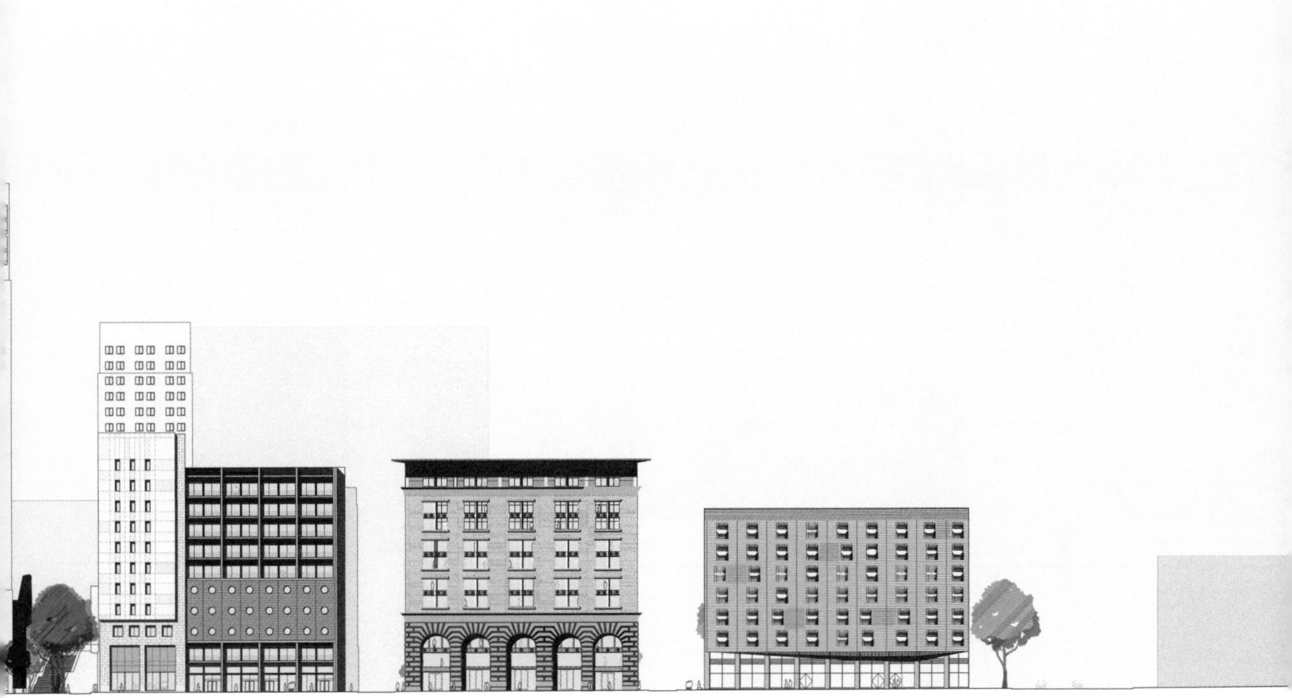

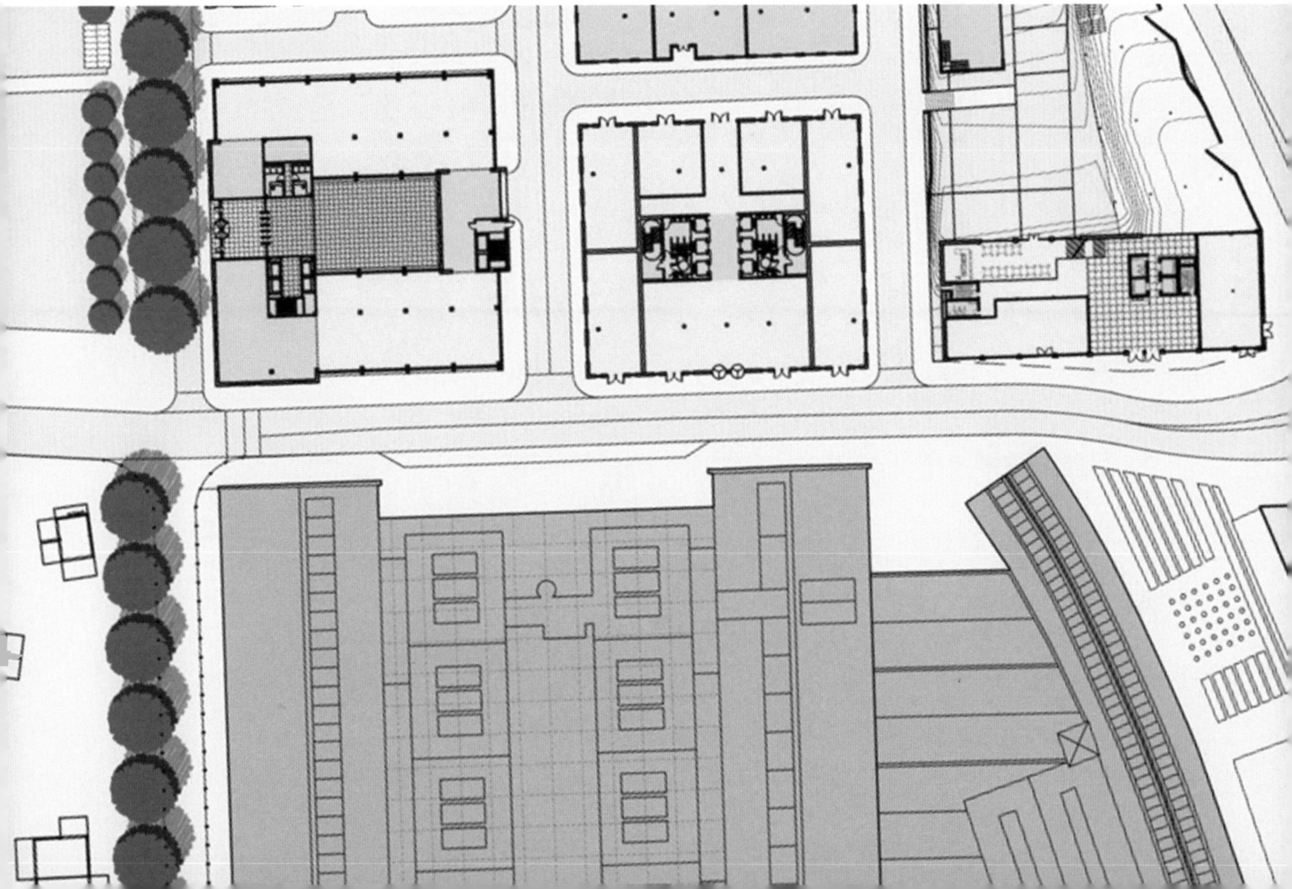

Discussion Peter Bishop: After having crawled around your model, I notice your siting of the Regent's Canal Tower has fundamentally changed the short and midrange views of Granary Square and the Regent's Canal. These spaces were completely dominated by the gasholders, but this tower breaks across that visual space. The gasholders were the objects that defined the character of the spaces around the Regent's Canal, and your tower has now altered that.

Alan Plattus: I think what is tantalizing here is that this almost looks like the group has established a set of common rules, because you see a kind of basic façade disposition that is echoed in each design. There is the beginning of a kind of collegiality about this group that makes it all the more fascinating when there are digressions from the norm. I think this is an important methodological point because one so rarely has the occasion for discussions where you can ask those kinds of questions. In other words, why your building might be different from the other buildings on that street suddenly becomes a meaningful question.

Graham Morrison: Did you think that when you were designing your individual buildings you were doing more than just designing buildings, or did you think you were participating in the making of a street?

Jaque Robertson: Your question is fundamental. All of us know the first two floors in good streets— the trees, the pavement, the shop windows, the lights—these things are everything. London is a city of good streets, trees, and squares. If this development is going to be planted, we need to know what it is going to look like.

David Partridge: The difficulty is you all have consistently presented these long elevations. We started the day talking about the character of the spaces, and yet we haven't seen a single drawing of a space as such. We have seen a lot of elevations, so our conversation has been focusing on those issues to the detriment of the public spaces.

Paul Finch: It never does any harm to show spaces you like. You know, there's nothing wrong with a bit of precedent.

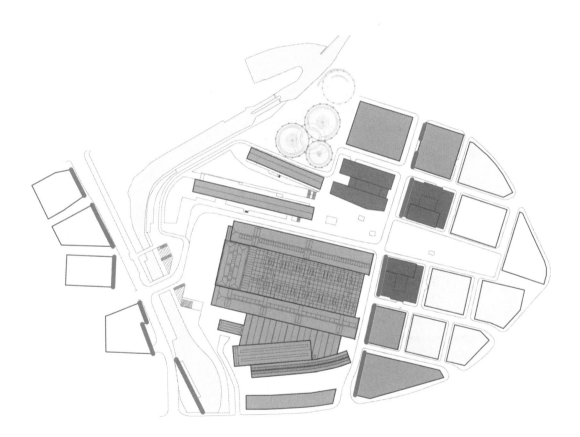

Plan diagram of Goods Street. The low heights of the existing historic buildings along Regent's Canal creates the opportunity for an urban dialogue between the taller Goods Street elevation (pink, right) and the Regent's Canal elevation (pink, left), while also offering a strong civic containment for the Granary, Coal Drops, and Gasholders that constitute the heart of King's Cross Central.

Model of the Goods Street scheme.

Massing study of Long Park seen from Granary Square. The long façades of the existing historic buildings lead the eye to a proposed pair of office buildings, which serve as a gateway to the park and frame the terminal tower element.

Rose Evans, Sini Kamppari, Aaron Taylor, and Neil Sondgeroth Long Park is located at the heart of the northern section of King's Cross Central and acts as the main organizational focus of the surrounding neighborhoods. The park also functions as the primary north-south pedestrian route of the site. Further, Long Park is the major green space of the master plan, and it is imagined as a quiet expanse that contrasts and complements the vibrant public life of the Boulevard and Regent's Canal.

As the main public space of the northern sector of King's Cross Central, our group felt Long Park needed a well-defined urban perimeter and an urban focal point. In addition to these requirements, we wanted the park to continue and reinforce the connectivity from old to new, which the student proposals for Goods Street enacted. Rather than be an "ending" to King's Cross Central, Long Park should promote a connection to the Triangle Site, an independent parcel of the master plan segregated from the main site by the busy traffic of York Way.

To provide a strong sense of containment for the park by the surrounding urban fabric, we created both a set of common datum heights and materials for the architectural organization of façades facing the park space. We also aimed to respond to the urban framing devices set up by the student proposals for Goods Street by reintroducing the idea of the urban frame, with two towers located at the northern terminus of the park. In this way it was our intention to open up the northern end of King's Cross Central with a new gateway rather than terminate it with a singular vertical element. We proposed a masonry viaduct through this new gateway that would take advantage of the change in grade elevation along York Way to connect directly with the Triangle Site. This viaduct was designed to recall both the historic Granary and Coal Drops buildings but also King's Cross and St. Pancras stations at the far opposite end of King's Cross Central. We hoped that by creating a new urban artifact that evokes the historic qualities of the site it might, in a visual and temporal sense, tie the northern and southern sections of the site together. By adding the viaduct, it was possible to realign the organization of the Triangle Site with a smaller third tower, thus reframing the thoroughfare of York Way with a third and culminating gateway motif.

top: Composite student east-elevation drawing of Long Park. middle: Composite student west-elevation drawing of Long Park. bottom: Composite student plan drawing of Long Park.

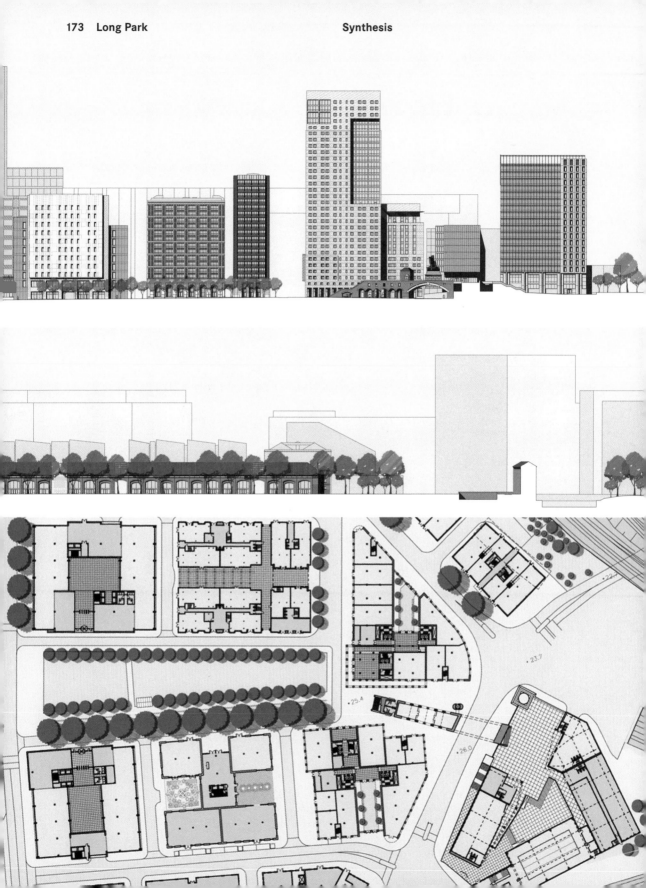

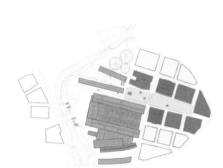

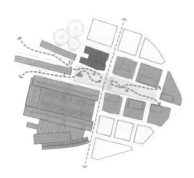

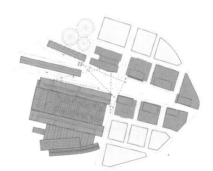

Plan diagrams of Long Park: (clockwise from top left) façade containment of green space, building-height intensity along the perimeter of the park, commercial (red), vehicular (yellow) and park (green) flow direction, site-line façade relationships from the Granary and Coal Drops buildings.

Discussion Peter Bishop: Was there any sort of conversation about the jump in scale from the transit sheds, which are relatively low, to the structures on Long Park, which are much taller?

Demetri Porphyrios: I think this site is an essentially archeological one, where found objects and new buildings intermingle. I am not sure that one has to be so delicate. This kind of juxtaposition of tiny buildings jammed up against much larger structures is what one finds in cities such as Rome, and it looks fantastic.

David Partridge: I am surprised that no one has talked about how to accommodate market housing in one location, intermediate housing in another, and subsidized housing in yet another. It seems to be a big problem with different types of units, different types of family occupation, and different types of social issues. These are all relevant issues that, while mainly about the requirements of management, also have an effect on the design of the buildings.

Robert Stern: I agree. How these different housing types change over time is also an issue for these kinds of plans. How one might reconfigure types based on the ebb and flow of the market has not been broached today.

Alan Plattus: Real estate aside, I do think Long Park as a whole has been successful in controlling the overall urban spatial aspect. There is a plausible level of coherence, and there is also a believable association of new development and existing structures. It is the kind of space people can identify with. Taking the point that Roger Madelin made earlier, I think people will come to be in Long Park for its urban experience rather than to see the buildings, and that is a good thing.

Patrick Bellew: I agree with all that, but this is such a powerful place in the site, this incredible framed view, so surely there must be enough value at the tower end. There isn't very much urban theater there in terms of level changes, public seating, or interaction with the tower base. Aside from the bridge it all seems quite bare. I think it was a missed opportunity.

Alan Plattus: One of the interesting questions urbanistically is, when you see the general progression of this district, you realize there has been a shift of gravity to this end of the site. This suggests that if you fill up these residential towers and offices, a row of retail and restaurants along Long Park would be quite attractive. This is a demonstration of the effects of critical mass at this end of the master plan.

Jaque Robertson: The end of the site is triangulated around the towers. It is quite powerful, and the triangulation of these vertical points of reference could be very elegant visually at the end of Long Park and at different points around the master plan. Instead of being the tail end of King's Cross Central, this collection of towers is turned into a head.

Model of the Long Park scheme.

from left: Richard Henley, Dean Robert A. M. Stern, student Sini Kamppari, Demetri Porphyrios, Alan Plattus, Paul Finch, Roger Madelin, and David Partridge discuss the Boulevard model during the final review.

from left: Vincent Scully, Patrick Bellew, Roger Madelin, and Peter Bishop, at student Seung Hwan Namgoong's final review.
page 182: Students Sini Kamppari (left) and Rose Evans (right) present their Goods Street scheme during the final review.

Architect and Developer Discussion Jaque Robertson: Architecture and urbanism are at their cores the same thing. You have to consider a building's façades and massing, the street space, and the infrastructure simultaneously. It cannot be done in sequence.

Alan Plattus: In light of this master plan, I realize the extent to which the planners have imbued it with a certain style. Even a master plan has style. I appreciate the students' struggle in façade-making as they responded to the urban spaces of the master plan in a positive way.

Tom Beeby: The relationship between planimetric formal order and style becomes interesting in the project. I think the loss of the ability of students to mine historical information is a serious problem both generally and during the review today. No one knows what the formal propositions are if they are unable to interpret history. I think this lies at the heart of today's struggles with elevations, plans, and urban spaces.

Ben Bolgar: There is a fear today that if we all learn a common language to create a dialogue, then we would all end up saying the same thing. This is utterly ludicrous. If you are able to have a dialogue through buildings, then this means there must be some basis of a common language and that you may depart from it as you think fit. If there is no common language, then you cannot create a civilized society because communication is not possible. That is the problem people find themselves in when they reject any sort of continuity.

Peter Bishop: I am quite intrigued by the lack of discussion about urban space and the lack of focus on buildings. When students engaged public space it had to do with landscape. One of the unifying elements is always going to be the landscape and the way it affects how these spaces work together. We had a really interesting debate about the streetscape, and I think it comes back to the image of King's Cross Central in the future. There is something about the street that is fundamental to the success of this development.

Richard Henley: This has been quite an interesting experiment because you've condensed into four months what would have taken five years—which is to have a lot of different architects cover a lot of ground. I was slightly disappointed with the proliferation of the façade as wallpaper theme. I wonder if one falls into the trap where just because anything is possible one can do anything one wants. You must not forget how to actually put things together in a structural sense.

Ben Bolgar: The arguments about monoculture versus what people have been referring to as the "zoo" are fascinating. We probably have a mistrust or phobia of huge, master-planned developments since there have been so many bad ones that seem to reflect our culture today. Perhaps in these presentations the variety is too great, but maybe the zoo-type development has some potential merits that have been overshadowed.

Patrick Bellew: I am interested in thinking about the extent to which you develop a code or culture to try and get a blending of styles against the idea of the zoo. In a world in which you can do whatever you like, the interesting question is what actually constitutes London in general and King's Cross Central in particular.

David Partridge: This studio has been very illuminating. Roger has pointed out to me how long it has been since we have done anything like this. I think it has brought home to us just how valuable it is to conduct exercises of this sort. In terms of the discussion about the zoo versus the controlling hand, you are right that there is a certain amount of mistrust. Exercises like this give us valuable lessons as we move forward with development.

Robert Evans: What we have seen in this discussion is the lack of a common language, even among a group of professionals, as to how to move forward and plan a good place. Through your work, this studio has raised a lot of issues we now need to think about.

Graham Morrison: I am grateful to the students for doing all of this work. I do think we are all the richer for it. The act of building is not just the act of making a building but the act of making all the spaces around the building. Do not be afraid of normality. In a way this is a very simple way of saying what Demetri has been stressing all along: Normality is not boring; it is an inherited existence. Normality is a way to describe the city that anyone who is not an architect understands.

Finally, although I am a modernist, I think that one thing modernism has to be condemned for is the erasing of the ability to compose, both in terms of the city plan and of façades. I think seeing you all struggle to make urban spaces and façades is really heartening because one needs to start somewhere.

Robert Stern: I would like to put in a word in defense of codes. Every building is governed by different sorts of codes. Most architecture has been affected by codes. It is true architects resist codes and that in this resistance creativity often has its greatest field of action. To say codes are constraining is not true. One needs to give people a set of ground rules by which to play the game.

Paul Finch: We have come up against the theme of codes several times today, from bar codes to self-coding, but I really think the spirit of the code is in a way the patronage strategy of the client coupled with actually getting together with the master planner or architect and working out what they want. Whether it is written out explicitly or if it is only an idea in their minds, the reality is that it is all built into the master plan—which, I must say, in this particular instance has proven to be quite robust despite the zoo approach to building design or lack of consideration for the street spaces. I think we can come away with a general sense of encouragement.

Demetri Porphyrios: In summary, thank you to the students, for your time and effort and for your suspension of disbelief. I would like to thank Argent and Roger for actually having the courage to do this studio. The studio shows the commitment of Yale to issues of urbanism and to the relationship of urbanism and architecture.

Student Khai Fung with Roger Madelin in London.

Roger Madelin's Observations What was fruitful in the studio was the way the students exhausted the process of integrating the design of buildings with urban plans and the various debates about character, iconic statements, place, and the difference between places. The contribution of the buildings' uses, architecture, and designs was exactly what the term was about, and I think there were interesting proposals. Some of the individual buildings contained ideas that we, as developers, thought were worth pursuing. Other students had ideas that could revisit areas in the master plan, not in a big way, but in an important way.

We have been in the middle of a site war and only procured the buildings in place seven years ago. Five years ago, after a huge amount of debate and criticism, we made a fairly concerted effort to think about design and place, and against which we tested the master plan, after a huge amount of debate and criticism. For the last two years we have been fighting the process to get the project through planning, and I was keen to stimulate this discussion in the Yale studio to raise it to another level. We have made decisions for development that will take place. At least we could pause for a bit and be informed about what we did and look at some of the work the students have done. After the final reviews I brought my colleagues together with Demetri Porphyrios and Allies & Morrison and discussed the issues and proposals that the students raised.

Every one of the students did something that was worthy of further thought. Lindsay Weiss's dramatic cantilevered building in the south would grab attention where ever it was placed, but most of the critics felt that it was clever there because that whole area has just happened by itself; it wasn't planned, there was infrastructure, but no one said, "Let's think about place, let's do infrastructure, and over the next decade more infrastructure will happen"—without any real ability to define what sort of place we have created. Most of us felt that Lindsay's intervention carried on what hadn't been designed but, by raising the building up and pointing out that this was an aggressive space, she gave more space back for the things that we want to do in this space, such as to sit and meet people. And the idea of the major retail building at that location was interesting.

Marko Maeno's thoughts and contributions to the Modern Terrace and how it is integrated or not integrated was provocative. Should it be on that side of the Boulevard? What is the role of the eastern end of the railway, and what happens at the northern end? Are there really two buildings? His presentation interrogated all these questions in the project.

Seung Hwan Namgoong's proposal for the little building by the petrol station is a gem of a building. We understand what he was trying to achieve, but we are not sure it would work there; nevertheless the reasons should be explored. His big building to the south of the canal raised some interesting issues about what this building should do and whether or not we should subdivide the building, perhaps, or should that piece of the square be different.

Khai Fung dealt with all four sides of a building that must perform well for both retail and office. Two sides have different jobs to do, but the building has to hold together—and he got that. In terms of an external envelope, no one really provided the character of the space. All of them were more or less successful to a greater or lesser degrees about building, but as to the southern area's character, everyone was left wondering about what kind of place it would be if you developed all the buildings as suggested. This situation was not unexpected; rather, it was the purpose of the term to raise those issues, and the panel of critics exposed those issues dramatically. There was a split between the North Americans and the Brits as to the design coding and the ability one had to control design aspects to a greater or lesser extent. Demetri's talk about the liberal society naturally led to debates about how much is a constraint and the sheer number of design rules that are put forward—all of which are issues that we discussed three years ago.

North of the King's Canal, Sini Kamppari's project used the buildings as bookends to the park. We liked the way her hotel building addressed and fronted the space. Further, in the future, we could come back and see that it is a fine building. It isn't shouting, but it is a long street where Lindsay also designed a project. Each building was well thought through in different styles, and it started a dialogue. Lindsay's subdued building design came across as not as important as the south side, which shouted. Rose Evan's idea of the taller building was a good idea. Khai Fung's program would be a good place to live. He thought carefully about where that building was situated and what kind of apartments would be there.

Aaron Taylor and Neil Sondgeroth worked together after midterm in the northeast area, identifying and resolving some of the issues better than we had. It was good to see a different approach. I felt proud of the great body of work, which can inspire a variety of ideas. The Yale studio's final crit woke us up and reinvigorated us.

Thomas Beeby is director of design for Hammond Beeby Rupert Ainge, Chicago. He has directed a diverse range of building projects including museums and libraries; university, theater, and performing-arts projects; urban and campus master plans; high-rise and suburban office buildings, renovations of historic structures; religious buildings; retail projects; housing developments, and private residences. Beeby was dean of the Yale School of Architecture from 1985 to 1991 and continues as adjunct professor of architecture. From 1980 to 1985 he was director of the school of architecture at the University of Illinois, Chicago, and was associate professor at the Illinois Institute of Technology from 1978 to 1980. Beeby lectures widely and has participated in numerous symposia including Yale's "Ineffable Space" in October 2007.

Patrick Bellew is a founding director of Atelier Ten, London, and is a chartered building services engineer with over twenty years of experience in the design of high-performance buildings and their systems. With extensive experience in the integration of environmental and building systems with architectural and structural schemes, Bellew has particular expertise in thermal-mass energy-storage technologies as well as radiant conditioning systems in projects around the world: Federation Square, Melbourne, Genzyme Building, Boston, the Kroon Building for the Yale School of Forestry, among others. In his field he is one of only three Honorary Fellows of the Royal Institute of British Architects.

Peter Bishop has been the director of design of London since 2007. In the mid-1980s he was the director of planning at Tower Hamlets and worked on developments and infrastructure projects including Spitalfields Market and Canary Wharf. In the mid-1990s he was director of property, architecture, and engineering at Haringey and also worked with the Broadwater Farm estate to re-establish the community after the 1980 riots. As director of environment at Hammersmith and Fulham, he worked on major development projects including the BBC, White City. He also worked with the Architecture Foundation on its first road show in the borough. Bishop joined Camden as director of culture and environmental services and successfully led the council's negotiations on the Kings Cross railway lands. He also worked very closely with UCL to commission urban design frameworks for Euston Road and Bloomsbury and negotiated the council's redevelopment of Swiss Cottage. He is a member of the English Heritage London Advisory Committee.

Ben Bolgar is the director of Design Theory & Networks at the Prince's Foundation for the Built Environment. In the past three years he has led multidisciplinary design workshops and teams for projects ranging in scale from new towns to single buildings focused on community and skills-building. He is also responsible for design advice to charities the Prince of Wales patronizes. As a practicing architect he has been responsible for the design and coordination of new residential and commercial buildings in the U.K. and abroad. Bolgar is a member of the Royal Institute of British Architects, a fellow of the Royal Society of Arts, and a trustee of the International Network for Traditional Building, Architecture, and Urbanism.

Robert Evans has been at Argent LPC since 2001, working on projects in Manchester and now directing the King's Cross project. Evans has worked as a planning and environmental consultant on defense, commercial, and infrastructure projects in the U.K., Canada, and Norway. He is a contributor to industry guidelines for Environmental Impact Assessment and a member of London First and Central London Partnership planning groups.

Paul Finch is editor of the *Architectural Review* and a member of the Commission for Architecture and the Built Environment (CABE) in London. He is also editorial director of the publishing group EMAP Construct. Finch was editor of the *Architects' Journal* from 1994 to 1999 and contributes to a wide range of forums as a commentator on architecture and design. In April 2004, after five years as chairman of CABE's design review committee, Finch moved to chair CABE's regional committee.

Richard Henley is an associate director of Arup and has been involved in the design, construction, and project management of engineering projects in the United Kingdom, the Middle East, Africa, Europe, and China. He is a chartered engineer and member of the Institution of Civil Engineers (U.K.). Henley was the designer and co-author of the Steel Construction Institute publication *102: Connections Between Steel and Other Materials*. He was co-author of a paper, "A Sensitive Application of Modern Engineering for the Tower of London," *Geo-Strata* (September/October 2007, volume 8, issue 5), of *The American Society of Civil Engineers*. Henley was a studio tutor at the Prince of Wales's Institute of Architecture from 1995 to 1997. He has been involved in the master-planning of King's Cross Central since the project's inception.

Graham Morrison began his architectural partnership with Robert Allies, Allies & Morrison, in 1984, a year after winning the competition for a new public square at the Mound, in Edinburgh. Completed commissions include the British Embassy, in Dublin, a major extension to the Horniman Museum, and the new BBC offices at White City, in London. Current commissions include three new faculty buildings for the University of Cambridge, the restoration and extension of the Royal Festival Hall, and the master plan for King's Cross. Over the last six years the firm has won numerous awards and participated in exhibitions including a touring retrospective. Morrison has served on committees of RIBA and Civic Trust, the Commission for Architecture & the Built Environment, and the London Advisory Committee of English Heritage

David Partridge joined Argent LPC in 1990 and is its joint chief executive. He is the architect of most of Argent's internal and external structures and relationships with joint-venture partners. He is also the first chairman of the Piccadilly Partnership (Manchester) Ltd. and chairman (designate) of the Manchester City Centre Management Company Ltd.

Alan Plattus has been professor at Yale since 1986, after serving on the faculty of Princeton University for seven years. He focuses his work on civic pageantry, the history of cities, and contemporary American architecture and urbanism. His consulting practice is working for the Stamford Urban Redevelopment Commission and the borough of Stonington, Connecticut. He founded and directs the Yale Urban Design Workshop and Center for Urban Design Research, which undertakes research and design studies for communities throughout Connecticut. He has served on the boards of the Association of Collegiate Schools of Architecture, the National Architectural Accrediting Board, and the *Journal of Architectural Education*.

Jaquelin Robertson, former dean of the School of Architecture at the University of Virginia and principal of Cooper Robertson Architects, in New York, has designed new communities at Daniel Island, South Carolina; New Albany, Ohio; Celebration and WaterColor, Florida; and Val d'Europe, France; a waterfront park, county courthouse, and the Visitor Reception and Transportation Center, in Charleston, South Carolina; the Henry Moore Sculpture Garden, in Kansas City; the Institute for the Arts & Humanities at the University of North Carolina, and Sony's Imageworks offices, in Culver City, California. He also prepared master plans for Monticello, Virginia, and the Battlefield Museum and the Visitor Center, at Gettysburg.

Robertson was a founder of the New York City Urban Design Group, the first director of the Mayor's Office of Midtown Planning and Development, and was a city planning commissioner. In 1975, he directed the planning and design of Iran's new capitol center, Shahestan Pahlavi. He received the Thomas Jefferson Foundation Medal in Architecture in 1998, the Seaside Institute Prize in 2002, and the Richard H. Driehaus Prize for Classical Architecture in 2007.

Vincent Scully is the Sterling Professor Emeritus of the History of Art and a Distinguished Visiting Professor, University of Miami. He has been on the Yale faculty since 1947. He has lectured all over the world and has served on numerous design juries. His books on art and architecture have earned international praise. He won the College Art Association Annual Book Award for *The Shingle Style* and the Society of Architectural Historians Annual Book Award for *The Architectural Heritage of Newport, Rhode Island, 1640–1915*. In 2000, Scully was the first recipient of the National Building Museum's Vincent Scully Prize, and in 2003 he was awarded the Urban Land Institute J. C. Nichols Prize for Visionaries in Urban Development.

Image Credits Argent Group PLC: 14, 18–19, 28–29, 42–43, 68, 72–73, 74; Argent Group PLC: © Anderson-Terzic 80–81; Argent Group PLC: © Simon Hazelgrove 52–53; Argent Group PLC: Townshend Landscape Architects © Quickbird Products 77; Camden Local Studies and Archives Centre: 48–49; Rose Evans: 124, 126, 127, 129; Khai Fung: 106, 109, 111, 146; Sini Kamppari: 82–85, 88–89 (with Lindsay Weiss), 118, 121, 123, 161, 162, 167, 170, 174; Mako Maeno: 100, 102–103, 105, 152–153; Seung Hwan Namgoong: cover, 112, 114–115 (with Arup), 117, 144–145 (with Khai Fung), 154, 158; Ordnance Survey on behalf of The Controller of Her Majesty's Stationery Office. Crown Copyright. All rights reserved. License No. AL 100036259: 44–45, 64, 69, 70–71, 79, 86–87; Porphyrios Associates: 15, 22–23, 34–35; Seung Hwan Namgoong, Khai Fung, Lindsay Weiss and Mako Maeno: 148–149, 156–157; Seung Hwan Namgoong, Khai Fung, Rose Evans, Lindsay Weiss Sini Kamppari, and Aaron Taylor: 164–165; Seung Hwan Namgoong, Khai Fung, Aaron Taylor, Sini Kamppari, Neil Sondgeroth, and Rose Evans: 172–173; Neil Sondgeroth: 48, 51, 54, 90–91, 138, 141, 142–143, 168–169 (with Aaron Taylor), 177, 178–179, 180–181, 182–183, 184; Aaron Taylor: 56, 57, 58–59, 60–61, 130, 132, 133, 135, 136–137; Lindsay Weiss: 92, 94–95, 97 (with Arup), 98–99, 150; White Star Publishers, Italy from Above Series (2007), © Marcello Bertinetti: 67.